Changing Labour Policies and Organization of Work in China

T0312175

The transformation of China's economy from a centrally planned to a market-oriented system has had a profound impact on management systems and practices at the firm level, particularly changes to the organization of work. One of the consequences of this is increasing social disparity reflected through inequality of employees' income and employment conditions. This book, based on extensive original research including interviews and questionnaire surveys in different regions of China, explores the exact nature of these changes and their effects. It examines state-owned enterprises, foreign-owned enterprises and domestic private enterprises, discusses the extent to which employees are satisfied with their employment conditions and whether they think their employment conditions are fair and outlines how managers and employees in China expect conditions to change in future.

Ying Zhu is Professor and Director of the Australian Centre for Asian Business, University of South Australia, Adelaide

Michael Webber is an Honorary Professor in the Department of Geography at Melbourne University

John Benson is a Professor in the School of Business at Monash University Malaysia and an Adjunct Professor in the Monash Business School, Monash University Australia

Routledge Studies in the Growth Economies of Asia

140. A Microcredit Alternative in South Asia
Akhuwat's experiment
Shahrukh Rafi Khan and Natasha Ansari

141. Development Agenda and Donor Influence in South Asia
Bangladesh's experiences in the PRSP regime
Mohammad Mizanur Rahman

142. How China's Silk Road Initiative is Changing the Global Economic Landscape
Edited by Yuan Li and Markus Taube

143. Trade Unions and Labour Movements in the Asia-Pacific Region
Edited by Byoung-Hoon Lee, Sek-Hong Ng and Russell Lansbury

144. International Entrepreneurship: A Comparative Analysis
Susan Freeman, Ying Zhu and Malcolm Warner

145. Ritual and Economy in Metropolitan China
A global social science approach
Carsten Herrmann-Pillath, Guo Man and Feng Xingyuan

146. Cyber Risk, Intellectual Property Theft and Cyberwarfare
Asia, Europe and the USA
Ruth Taplin

147. Changing Labour Policies and Organization of Work in China
Impact on firms and workers
Ying Zhu, Michael Webber and John Benson

For more information about this series, please visit: https://www.routledge.com/asianstudies/series/SE0133

Changing Labour Policies and Organization of Work in China

Impact on Firms and Workers

Ying Zhu, Michael Webber, and John Benson

LONDON AND NEW YORK

First published 2021
by Routledge
2 Park Square, Milton Park, Abingdon, Oxon OX14 4RN

and by Routledge
52 Vanderbilt Avenue, New York, NY 10017

Routledge is an imprint of the Taylor & Francis Group, an informa business

British Library Cataloguing-in-Publication Data
A catalogue record for this book is available from the British Library

Library of Congress Cataloging-in-Publication Data
A catalog record has been requested for this book

ISBN: [978-1-138-31742-0] (hbk)
ISBN: [978-0-429-45522-3] (ebk)

Typeset in TimesNewRoman
by MPS Limited, Dehradun

Contents

List of illustrations   vi
Authors   viii
Preface   x
Acknowledgements   xi
List of abbreviations   xii

1   Economic and social reform in China   1

2   Policy reforms, employment relations and
    labour management   11

3   Management initiatives on work and
    labour management   27

4   Employees' experiences and responses to labour
    management reform   45

5   Regular workers and perceptions of fairness   61

6   Well-being and satisfaction among workers   81

7   Future expectations among workers   106

8   Conceptualizing the economy of labour
    beyond markets   126

9   The ongoing challenges of labour management
    reform in China   144

Bibliography   157
Index   166

List of Illustrations

Tables

1.1 The economic profile of selected regions, 2018   6
1.2 Profile of respondents by location   7
3.1 Managers' responses to labour management reform in China   40
4.1 Employees' responses to labour management reform
    and management practices in China   55
5.1 Research themes and worker survey questions   66
5.2 Employees' perceived fairness and satisfaction with jobs
    and working conditions by region (%)   68
5.3 Employees' overall perceived fairness and satisfaction
    with jobs and working conditions (%)   69
6.1 Research themes and worker survey questions   85
6.2 Employees' general and relative health (%)   88
6.3 Employees' current satisfaction with work (%)   89
6.4 Employees' satisfaction with work five years ago relative
    to the present (%)   91
6.5 Employees' well-being and satisfaction (%)   93
7.1 Employees' expectations concerning their current job
    over the next five years (%)   109
7.2 Workers' comments regarding employment prospects in
    their current job   111
7.3 Employees' expectations if they lost their current job (%)   115
7.4 Workers' comments regarding employment prospects if
    they lost their current job   116
7.5 Employees' optimism concerning employment improvements
    over the next five years (%)   119
9.1 Macro-economic reform, management and worker responses,
    and impact on employee well-being and expectations   145

Figure

1.1 Conceptual framework of the book   2

Authors

Ying Zhu is Professor and Director of the Australian Centre for Asian Business at the University of South Australia. He was born in Beijing and graduated from Peking University with a Bachelor of International Economics in 1984. Ying then worked as an economist at Shenzhen Special Economic Zone in China for four years between 1984 and 1988. He completed a PhD on the role of export processing zones in East Asian development, focusing on South Korea, Taiwan, China and Thailand, at the University of Melbourne between 1989 and 1992. Subsequently, he worked at Victoria University and the University of Melbourne for 17 years. Ying has published widely in the areas of international HRM, international business and economic development in Asia. He has published numerous articles and books. Ying's most recent monographs are *Improving Competitiveness through Human Resource Development in China: The Role of Vocational Education* (Routledge, 2020) with Min Min; *Business Leaders and Leadership in Asia* (Routledge, 2017) with Ren Shuang, Ngan Collins and Malcolm Warner; *Conducting Business in China and India: A Comparative and Contextual Analysis* (Palgrave Macmillan, 2017) with Sardana Deepak; *Employers' Association in Asia: Employer Collective Action* (Routledge, 2017) with John Benson and Howard Gospel; and *Strategic Human Resource Management in China: A Multiple Perspective* (Routledge, 2017) with Min Min and Mary Bambacas.

Michael Webber is Professor Emeritus, School of Geography at the University of Melbourne. After undergraduate and graduate training at Cambridge University and the Australian National University, he has held positions in the departments of geography at the ANU, McMaster University and the University of Melbourne and visiting positions at the universities of Cincinnati, Bristol, Sydney, Minnesota, UCLA and Monash. An economic geographer, Michael's research combines formal social theory and large-scale, survey-based empirical methods to identify how people's working lives are affected by international political and social processes; this includes an interest in environment and development. His recent research focuses on the economic and geographic transformation of modern China and the management of water in China. He has published 15 books and over

100 academic papers. Michael has consulted to government departments, trade unions and non-government organizations and is a Fellow of the Academy of the Social Sciences in Australia.

John Benson is Professor in the School of Business at Monash University Malaysia and an Adjunct Professor in the Department of Management, Monash Business School, Australia. His major research interests include Japanese management and unions, economic reform in China, employee voice, knowledge work and generations and diversity in the workplace. John is a Fellow of the Academy of the Social Sciences in Australia and has published over 120 academic papers and 14 books. His most recent authored monographs are *Teacher Management in China: The Transformation of Educational Systems* (Routledge, 2016) with Eva Huang and Ying Zhu and *The Political Economy of New Regionalism in Northeast Asia: Dynamics and Contradictions?* (Routledge, 2018) with Chang Jae Lee, You-il Lee, Ying Zhu and Yoon-Jong Jang. Recent edited monographs include *Employers' Associations in Asia* (Routledge, 2017) with Ying Zhu and Howard Gospel and *Dispute Resolution in Islamic Finance: Alternatives to Litigation?* (Routledge, 2019) with Adnan Trakic and Pervaiz Ahmed.

Preface

China has changed dramatically over the past four decades. Looking back in 2020, it is hard to visualize the business world of the 'old' China that grew out of the socialist state. Beginning in 1979 with the first tentative move towards restructuring of the economy and the reform of state-owned enterprises, China has attracted global attention for its rapid modernization and transformation of the economy. It was clearly taken as a given that macro-economic reform would lead to enterprise-level reform and a transition from a centrally planned economy to what was described by many as a market-oriented socialist state.

It was in that context that we published *The Everyday Impact of Economic Reform in China: Management Change, Enterprise Performance and Daily Life* (Routledge: London and New York) in 2010. The underlying goal of that book was to trace the impact of the economic restructuring and reform on the way enterprises conducted their human resource management and employment relations, and how such changes affected enterprise performance, the quality of working life and ultimately households and families. The findings of that research suggested that 25 years after the reform process had commenced, the macro-level reform had led to enterprise-level improvements in incomes, working conditions and the quality of working life. Workers and their families enjoyed these benefits, although rising prices, especially housing, and occupational and urban/rural wage differentials meant that many workers and their families had gained little.

An important consequence of the prolonged period of economic reform was the increasing social disparity as reflected in workers' income and employment conditions. We therefore sought to understand what was taking place in the following decade and to analyze in a more qualitative and intuitive way what the responses were at the macro-economic level and how this played out at the enterprise level. We were particularly interested in enterprise and workers' response to the reform agenda, as well as workers' perceptions of fairness, well-being and concerns about the future. Our research challenged many of the approaches adopted by labour market scholars and this also led us to consider new ways of conceiving labour markets in what could be a dynamic, but at times, chaotic environment.

Ying Zhu, Michael Webber and John Benson,
August 2020

Acknowledgements

We would first and most importantly like to thank the managers and workers who participated in this study. Without their patience and understanding, this book would not have been possible. We would also like to acknowledge and thank our partners in China: Professor Zhao Wei at Beijing Normal University and Professor Xie Yuhua at Hunan University, who directed the interviews and surveys so thoroughly and assisted us in a multitude of tasks. We would also like to record our appreciation of the excellent work of Dr Min Min and Ms Marina Morgan in carrying out the data analysis and the editing of the manuscript. The research was funded through an Australian Research Council Discovery Grant which allowed for a more detailed and in-depth study than otherwise would have been the case. Finally, but not least, we would like to thank the University of South Australia, the University of Melbourne and Monash University (Australia and Malaysia) for their ongoing support of the project.

Abbreviations

ACFTU	All China Federation of Trade Unions
CCP	Chinese Communist Party
CSR	Corporate social responsibility
COE	Collectively owned enterprise
DPE	Domestic-private enterprise
FDI	Foreign direct investment
FIE	Foreign-invested enterprise
GDP	Gross domestic product
HR	Human resources
HRM	Human resource management
HMT	Hong Kong, Macao and Taiwan
HPWS	High performance work systems
IMF	International Monetary Fund
JV	Joint venture
JSC	Joint-stock company
KPI	Key performance indicator
MES	Modern enterprise system
MOLSS	Ministry of Labour and Social Security
OH&S	Occupational health and safety
RMB	Renminbi – the official Chinese currency with the yuan being the principal unit. One yuan was equal to 0.14 (USD), 0.22 (AUD) and 0.12 (GBP) as on 14 May 2020.
SEZ	Special economic zone
SOE	State-owned enterprise
WTO	World Trade Organization

1 Economic and social reform in China

Introduction

Over the past four decades, China has implemented extensive economic and social reform which has transformed the economy from a centralized planning arrangement to a market-oriented system with increasing enterprise autonomy (Zhu, Webber and Benson, 2010). At the heart of the economic reform were changes to economic and labour policy at the macro level and the restructuring of management systems and practices at the firm level, particularly changes to the management of labour. This economic reform and the consequent changes not only have had a significant influence on the society and enterprises, but also have impacted on individual employees' work life.

Earlier assessments of the impact of this reform have been generally positive for workers and many workers have had increases in their income, improved working conditions and an enhanced quality of working life (see Zhu, Webber and Benson, 2010). These benefits have not, however, been spread equally among workers and more generally members of the wider society. One of the consequences of this outcome is the increasing social disparity reflected through inequality of employees' income and employment conditions (Zhu, Warner and Feng, 2011). Conservative estimates of the Gini coefficient for China, a measure of social inequality, show that the coefficient rose from 0.43 in 1990 to 0.475 in 2016 (NBS, 2017). This rate is generally regarded as above the 'dangerous' point of 0.40 for maintaining political, social and economic stability (Tobin, 2011).

Whilst such inequality does not happen in a vacuum, and many factors underpin and contribute to this imbalance, it is equally clear that enterprise-level reform plays a major role in the working lives and general satisfaction levels of employees. The potential impact of these enterprise-level reforms raises further questions around the sustainability of the reform process in China at both the societal and the workplace level. In this book, we will focus on the enterprise, although we recognize that societal factors directly and indirectly interact with workplaces. We will, therefore, take a broad approach to addressing the key questions presented below and the conclusions that are drawn.

Our conceptual framework of analysis utilized in this book is illustrated in Figure 1.1. Economic and market reform directly impacts on the enterprise, in particular on the way it is structured and the way it manages labour (Zhu, Webber and Benson, 2010). The first question we thus seek to address is: what have been the key economic, legal and industrial policy reforms implemented over this time and how have they directly impacted on the management of labour? Reforms, however, require action on the part of various parties, in this case enterprise managers and workers or employees. Thus, our second question is: how have management and workers responded to these reforms and influenced the management of labour and the operations of the enterprise? This leads to our third question, namely: what have been the specific effects on pay, conditions of work (e.g. working time, job security, social insurance, welfare and other benefits) and the opportunities for promotion, training and future development? Even if we find wages and working conditions have improved, the critical issue in understanding the impact on society is whether employees are generally satisfied with their current employment conditions and jobs; that is, do workers perceive the reforms to have led to reasonably fair distribution of outcomes and to have been beneficial to their work and social life?

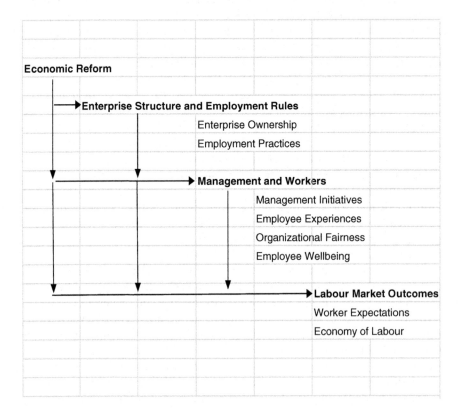

Figure 1.1 Conceptual framework of the book.

Exploring the above questions will tell us much about the past impact of economic reform although we are also interested in this book to understand the future effects of such reform. Thus, a further question we will address is: how have the changing policies and labour management affected the well-being of employees, their level of work satisfaction, their feelings of equity and their expectations for the future? Finally, we know that inequality in China has increased and many commentators have suggested various reasons for this. Given this book's focus on labour policy and the management of labour, the final question to be addressed will be: how can labour management and markets best be conceptualized in China and can such theory have application beyond China?

The aim of this book is to address the questions illustrated in Figure 1.1 by using our recent research in China to extend our earlier work on labour management and employment relations. We do this by tracing the impact of reforms at the policy level and changes to labour management work at the firm level and, in turn, the effect on employees (see Zhu, Webber and Benson, 2010). By using the various literatures on policy reform, the management of labour, and the relations between transformation at macro and firm levels, as well as disparities, (un)fairness and (dis)satisfaction at the worker level, the book seeks to integrate the literature and to locate the study of China within the main currents of Western discourse, while recognizing the potential location-specific aspects of the research site.

Changes to the management of labour

As outlined and examined in Chapter 2, considerable reform has taken place in China since the economic transition process started in 1979. This has been discussed in detail elsewhere (Zhu, Webber and Benson, 2010). Building on this earlier work, Chapter 2 will thus provide a commentary on more recent reforms with a particular focus on labour management at the firm level.

Prior to the commencement of economic reform, Chinese labour management was characterized by the central allocation of labour, strict adherence to rules and regulations, the provision of standardized wages and extensive prescribed working conditions, and a range of social benefits, including housing, schooling and recreational activities. Often referred to as the 'iron-rice bowl' or a 'cradle to the grave' mentality, such an approach was mandated by government and executed through state-owned enterprises (SOEs). Profit was not a driving force and many SOEs were technically loss-making ventures. This approach was possible as long as the individual SOEs met their production quota (Zhu, Webber and Benson, 2010).

Following the opening of the Chinese economy, many SOEs, particularly those with a less strategic role, were subsequently abandoned and had to fend for themselves with little or no state support. Dramatic changes at the enterprise level ensued, including the need for enterprises to become profitable and for workers to adopt new labour management practices. In so doing, it was hoped that the enterprises would be competitive, both domestically and, in some cases, internationally. This early period in the transition of Chinese industry to a 'socialist market economy' also witnessed the rise of alternative enterprise structures, including township and village enterprises, privately owned domestic companies, foreign firms and joint-stock companies (JSCs).

These new enterprise forms, along with changes to government employment and labour market policies, heralded a new era for the way firms managed labour. Wages increased significantly, more contemporary human resource management (HRM) practices were introduced and generally working conditions improved (Zhu, Webber and Benson, 2010). Accompanying such changes were tighter controls on workers, more demanding production targets and generally higher levels of accountability and responsibility (Benson and Zhu, 1999).

Importantly, running parallel to such changes, three transitional negative effects on workers were beginning to emerge. First, the benefits of the 'iron-rice bowl' began to diminish. No longer could enterprises take a life-long approach to employee welfare; benefits such as the provision of housing, schooling and recreation facilities were gradually reduced and, in many cases, discontinued. Second, improved worker performance and flexibility became increasingly a focus for management (Benson, Debroux, Yuasa and Zhu, 2000). Performance-related pay, whilst often leading to an increase in wages, also meant that the work intensity increased as well as the adoption of new work processes and practices. For older workers, retraining was essential, but also posed difficulties for them as they had become accustomed to a different approach to work. Third, at a societal level, the general increase in the cost of living, the decline in the availability of cheap housing (often close to work), the increasing cost of transport to travel to the workplace and the substantial disadvantages faced by the considerable number of domestic migrant workers (lack of schooling for children, lower wages, limited availability of various insurances) meant that not all workers shared in the gains from the economic reform agenda. In turn, pressure was placed on the state to avoid further discontent that could lead to wider social disorder.

Research methodology

In addressing the questions outlined in the preceding section, the book will focus on various types of enterprises (different categories of enterprise have different characteristic modes of labour management), various regions (reform and marketization have proceeded at different rates in different parts of the country) and various characteristics of workers (different categories of workers face specific challenges in the employment policies of enterprises). By adopting this methodology, the findings of the research will provide a reasonable representation of Chinese enterprises and allow valid conclusions to be drawn. The immensity and complexity of China, however, mean that for any particular group of workers, firm type or enterprise location, variations will exist, and thus any wider inferences need to be treated with caution.

Research design

Given the limited research in China on the above-mentioned issues and the need to examine the contextual implications, we designed and conducted structured qualitative/quantitative surveys targeting managers and various groups of employees working in different types of enterprises in terms of ownership structure and location. Targeting such a diverse group of enterprises, managers and workers enabled us to adopt a more holistic approach to our investigations into employees' perceptions of enterprise policies and management systems and to compare similar and different responses towards fairness across enterprises (Hesse-Biber and Leavy, 2011; Miles, Huberman and Saldana, 2014).

Sample and procedures

Our sample was drawn predominantly from different types of enterprises, from different regions and from employees with different characteristics, skills and positions. Predominantly, four types of enterprises were sampled: SOEs, domestic-private enterprises (DPEs), foreign-invested enterprises (FIEs) and JSCs. Not all enterprises fell neatly into these categories, although, in general, the analysis will focus on these four types. These enterprise types range from the pre-reform enterprises that were being forced to change to enterprises representing the new forces in the market economy. Our sample was drawn from two regions of China which we refer to loosely as North China (Beijing and Hebei) and South China (Hunan and Guangdong). These regions and provinces were chosen as they present different political, economic and social environments. Some key economic details of these regions are presented in Table 1.1.

Among these four regions, Beijing is the capital of China and the country's political and cultural centre. The other three regions are also important, but in other ways. For example, Guangdong was one of the earliest provinces adopting the 'open door' policies, with three of the four initial special economic zones being located in this region (i.e. Shenzhen, Zhuhai and Shantou). This province has now become the leading area for advanced manufacturing and high-tech industries. Hebei and Hunan are inland provinces with a strong focus on agriculture and mass manufacturing sectors.

In terms of economic strength, Guangdong is in the leading position in most relevant economic indicators, including total GDP, GDP per capita, total trade value and retail sales of consumer goods. Given Beijing's unique

Table 1.1 The economic profile of selected regions, 2018

Key economic indicators	Beijing	Hebei	Hunan	Guangdong
Population (millions)	21.54	75.56	96.05	113.46
GDP (US $, billions)	433	514	520	1,390
GDP per capita (US $)	20,096	6,803	5,414	12,251
Industry sector (% of GDP)				
	0	9	8	4
• Primary	19	45	40	42
• Secondary	81	46	52	56
• Tertiary				
Trade values (US $, billions)	369	54	47	1,085
	31	34	31	647
• Exports	338	20	16	438
• Imports				
Retail sales of consumer goods (US $, millions)	1,678	2,364	2,234	5,643
Life expectancy (age in years)	80	75	75	77

Source: NBS, National Data, 2019.

position as the national capital, it is the second largest first-tier city in terms of GDP in China. It is home to the headquarters of most of China's largest state-owned companies and has the largest number of Fortune Global 500 companies in the country (BSY, 2018). Beijing has become the base of the post-industrial Chinese economy and, at 81 per cent of GDP, has the largest tertiary sector as a proportion of GDP among all Chinese cities. Sector-wise, Beijing has highly developed financial, service, R&D, cultural and education industries. Specifically, the added value of Beijing's modern service industry – which includes financial, technology, information services and other advanced services – accounted for around 60 per cent of GDP in 2018. Income derived from cultural industries, meanwhile, reached $15 billion in that year (Y. Z. Zhang, 2019).

The remaining two provinces, namely, Hebei and Hunan, have a relatively high concentration of primary and secondary sectors contributing towards total GDP in comparison with Beijing and Guangdong. In addition, they have relatively lower levels of GDP per capita, international trade values and retail sales of consumer goods. These figures illustrate that these two regions are less developed economically in comparison with Beijing and Guangdong. The different life expectancies among the four regions also are consistent with the level of economic development with overall figures of 80 years for Beijing, 77 years for Guangdong and 75 years for both Hebei and Hunan provinces.

With the support of our local partner institutions (Beijing Normal University and Hunan University), we targeted 30 enterprises in each location (north and south) and 10 employees in each enterprise. Enterprises were chosen, as outlined earlier, to represent various forms of ownership and within them employee characteristics, skills and positions. In total, 605 employees completed the questionnaire: 297 from the north and 308 from the south. This sample size was felt to be sufficient to explore in detail the constructs of interest and to be reasonably representative of the employees in each region.

As summarized in Table 1.2, the age of participants ranged from 20 to 55 years, with the majority aged below 35 years. Over 80 per cent of respondents were regular contract employees with the remainder being

Table 1.2 Profile of respondents by location

Demographic background	North (Beijing and Hebei, total 297)		South (Hunan and Guangzhou, total 308)	
	Number of employees	%	Number of employees	%
Worker type				
Dispatched	5	2	55	18
Contract workers	291	98	253	82
Age				
<35 years old	214	72	207	67
35–45 years	58	20	58	19
>45 years old	35	18	43	14
Gender				
Male	132	44	197	64
Female	165	56	111	36
Education				
Tertiary and above	136	45	134	43
Below tertiary	161	55	174	56
Local Hukou status				
Yes	189	64	153	50
No	108	36	155	50
Urban/rural citizen				
Urban	209	70	186	61
Rural	88	30	122	39
Professional certification				
Yes	127	43	177	58
No	170	57	131	42
Enterprise ownership				
SOE	87	29	107	35
Private domestic enterprise (PDE)	111	37	91	30
FIE	77	26	57	18
JSC	11	4	0	0
Others[*]	11	4	53	17

Source: Worker survey.

Note
[*] 'Others' includes Hong Kong (HK), Macao and Taiwan investment companies.

dispatched or subcontract employees. Workers' tenure ranged from 3 to 15 years, with 55 per cent being graduates of high or vocational schools. The remaining sizeable minority (45 per cent) were graduates of tertiary institutions. The participants' job roles were varied and included manual workers, salespeople, IT professionals, HR specialists, financial/accounting clerks, team leaders and operations managers.

Data analysis

The data was analyzed in accordance with the key research themes presented earlier in this chapter. As such, we dissected the data based on employee profiles, such as differences in age, gender, educational qualifications, household registration backgrounds (i.e. local vs. migrant status and urban vs. rural citizen) and professional/occupational certification. We also considered enterprise location, worker type (dispatched vs. regular contract) and enterprise ownership. These variables are presented in Table 1.2. Such characteristics have the potential to explain many of the different experiences and perceptions of employees concerning economic reform in China. For example, skilled and professional employees would generally have higher incomes and would be moving towards middle-class status compared with less skilled manual employees and, in particular, rural migrant labour.

Design and structure of the book

Figure 1.1 presented earlier in this chapter provides a conceptual framework for the underpinning analysis of this book. Macro-economic reform in China over the past four decades has significantly influenced the structure of enterprises and the way they manage labour. This is most clearly seen in the ownership structure of the enterprise and its employment practices. At this micro-economic or enterprise level, these strategies are modified by the responses of management and labour to such macro-economic reform. We contend that such a process leads to certain intended and unintended outcomes which then influence workers' perceptions of fairness and well-being. Such perceptions will shape workers' future expectations as well as question the relevance of the theoretical approaches to analyzing such labour market outcomes. Although the model is relatively simple to understand, it becomes quite complex to explore as it is shaped by a variety of initiatives by management and responses by workers and ultimately is perceived in quite different ways by workers in the normal course of their work and social lives.

The structure of the book replicates the sequential flow of this model. The book comprises nine chapters, including an introduction and conclusion. Chapter 1, the present chapter, provides a brief discussion on China's economic reform with a focus on the changes in the management of labour at the enterprise level. Such changes are influenced by policy reforms, the influence of the state and the institutional, legal and general environment of business operations. These are discussed in Chapter 2. This introductory chapter also outlines the key questions to be addressed, as well as providing details on the research design and methodology.

Chapter 2, as alluded to above, provides a detailed commentary on economic and market reforms, with a particular focus on the past decade. These reforms are placed in the institutional, legal and general environment of business operations within the broad areas of employment relations and labour management. The influence of the state and the responses from enterprise management are critical in this process. The chapter concludes with a discussion on the implications for labour management.

The next two chapters expand on this process by exploring in more detail management initiatives (Chapter 3) and the responses from workers (Chapter 4) which may consolidate or modify such changes to labour management. In these transitions to the modern, contemporary organization, enterprises will need to undertake a variety of actions, such as addressing skill and labour shortages through a variety of HRM strategies which will include wages, welfare and benefits as well as developing the organizational culture and creatively managing labour relations (Chapter 3). Workers, for their part, will need to respond to such management initiatives, individually and collectively. Such responses will involve a clear assessment of policy changes and may well impact on macro-reform policies and micro-reform implementation (Chapter 4).

Chapters 5 and 6 then explore workers and their perceptions of fairness and well-being. Chapter 5 considers the various forms of justice or fairness at the workplace (procedural, distributive and interactional) as well as overall job satisfaction. Chapter 6 extends these findings to a consideration of employee health and job stress, the nature of the job (tasks, job responsibility, accountability and participation in management), and a range of attitudinal issues that indicate perceptions around workloads, supervisor and co-worker support, and organizational commitment. These findings are broken down by location, types of enterprises and jobs, and a range of employee demographics. In doing so, these chapters attempt to illustrate how macro-level reform can result in micro- or enterprise-level consequences that can directly impact on the efficiency and effectiveness of the economic transition and identify some of the key impediments to the change.

Chapters 7 and 8 conclude the substantive chapters of the book. Chapter 7 explores future expectations among workers and discusses how policy changes and management strategy will need to take into consideration workers' expectations for the future. This matching of central planning to individual and group needs will be essential to avoid the possibility of large-scale disruption, not only at the workplace but also within the wider society. Chapter 8 provides a more theoretical discussion which utilizes the experiences and findings of our fieldwork for this project and the findings of our many years of research on China. We challenge conventional, deterministic theories and approaches to labour markets based on the ongoing changes in China which lead to an alternative concept that we have termed the 'economy of labour'. This argument progresses by discussing the deficiencies of conventional labour market approaches and proposing a new way of thinking about the ways in which work is sought and offered.

Chapter 9 provides a conclusion to the book focusing on trends and implications of the macro- and micro-level reform processes. Commencing with a summary of the research findings, the chapter then discusses the theoretical implications as well as the empirical outcomes discovered in the course of the research. Recommendations for future research concludes the chapter.

2 Policy reforms, employment relations and labour management

Introduction

This chapter reviews policy reforms and the developments in employment relations and labour management since 2010. In order to provide a historical context, the chapter will commence with some comments on reform prior to this date, much of which can be found in '*The Everyday Impact of Economic Reform in China: Management Change, Enterprise Performance and Daily Life*' (Zhu, Webber and Benson, 2010: 10; 14–15). In China, policy reforms have been carried out and implemented by changing some existing policies as well as developing new policies, laws and regulations that are expected to be taken as the new policies and legal norms. In this chapter, we illustrate the influence of governments at different levels on policy changes, the rationale and purpose of new legislations, the implications for changing organization of work and the responses from relevant stakeholders, namely, business owners and managers as well as workers and their representatives.

The issues discussed in this chapter follow the priority of government policy and regulatory initiatives, namely, 1) managing labour disputes and controlling labour unrest to achieve 'social harmony', 2) coping with the ongoing changes in labour supply due to the demographic changes (e.g. ageing population) and other factors, such as regional competition for talent, increasing labour costs and shifting of industrial structure, 3) managing wage increases and creating new job opportunities and 4) developing a comprehensive social insurance system. After reviewing these key policy initiatives, the chapter then focuses on the implications for business owners and managers as well as workers and their representatives, namely, the trade unions. The time period being covered in this part of the historical review includes the entire 12th national five-year plan period between 2011 and 2015 as well as the major part of the 13th national five-year plan period between 2016 and 2020. Hence, our focus will be on changes during the first five-year period, complemented with more information on recent years.

Policy and regulatory initiatives for managing labour disputes and labour unrests

The first three decades of economic reform

Economic reform began in early 1978 when the state, through the CCP's Central Party Committee, refocused national economic policy from the so-called 'continuation of class struggle' to a policy of 'socialist economic construction'. The reform started in rural areas with the People's Commune system being replaced by the responsibility system (Hsu, 1991; Riskin, 1988). This was followed by reform of the fiscal system with a shift from state controls on enterprise investment and profits to an emphasis on enterprise autonomy in decisions concerning investments and the allocation of after-tax profits (Wong, 1995; Blejer, 1991; Li, 1991). A new banking and financial system was introduced with the goal of establishing a commercial banking system which would include a central bank, commercial banks and a variety of other financial institutions and companies (Yang, 1995; World Bank, 1988). At the same time, the economy was opened up in order to stimulate international trade and foreign investment in China through the creation of Special Economic Zones (SEZs), Open Cities and Open Regions (Webber and Zhu, 1995). This policy was focused on the east coast regions but was subsequently extended to the entire country (Lardy, 1994; World Bank, 1994, 1997; Sheahan, 1986; Kleinberg, 1990).

At the enterprise level, these macro-level policy initiatives provided State-owned enterprises (SOEs) with increasing freedom to independently conduct their affairs, although the initiatives also heralded the decline in financial support from the state. Only the largest SOEs or those important to the strategic interests of the government gained some reprieve from this policy. The policy shift led to a variety of business forms emerging and the relaxation of the prescribed ways enterprises could manage their workers. These were significant changes in the nature of the Chinese enterprise and necessitated new or revised statutes and directives to regulate employment (including women's work), employment relations and trade unions as the economy transitioned to a market economy. These new and revised laws covered most economic entities, including SOEs, Domestic private enterprises (DPEs) and Foreign invested enterprises (FIEs).

The major legislative developments that impacted labour management and employment relations during the first three decades were as follow:

1   The *Fixed-term Contract Employment* regulation was introduced in 1986 which stipulated that all future employment would be on the basis of short-term fixed contracts. This contrasted with the jobs-for-life principle that existed for most of the period from 1949.

2   A range of gender-related legislation was introduced to protect the rights and health of women. These included the *Female Workers' Labour*

Protection Legislation (1988), *Prohibited Posts for Female Workers* (1990) and the *Protection of Women' Rights and Interests* (1992).

3 Administrative reforms were undertaken in 1992 to improve the system of labour administration, wage distribution and social insurance. These reforms were jointly proposed and agreed between the Commission for Restructuring the Economy, the Ministry of Labour and the All China Federation of Trade Unions (ACFTU).

4 The *Provision of Settlement of Surplus Labour* was introduced in 1993, providing guidelines for enterprises that wished to reduce their labour force through such means as the creation of new jobs, retraining and a variety of leave arrangements. Enterprises' liability for their workers was not, however, reduced. Accompanying this reform was a system of unemployment insurance for dismissed workers.

5 A new *Labour Law* was introduced in 1995 which provided a framework for the conduct of enterprise-level industrial relations. This legislation incorporated the minimum wage regulations of 1993 as well as permitting collective bargaining and the formation of trade unions. This law applied to all enterprises irrespective of their structure or ownership and was aimed at protecting the rights of workers while promoting economic development and social progress. The Act also widened the system of labour contracts, outlined policy on occupational health and safety, employment of juveniles, vocational training, social insurance and welfare, and the settlement of industrial disputes.

6 The 1950 *Trade Union Law* was revised in 1992 (and again in 2001), specifying the organizational structure of trade unions and defining their rights and obligations. This law was premised on the need for the management of SOEs and trade union officials to work together for the common good of the state. Nevertheless, the law recognized the potential for conflict in a range of areas, including negotiating collective agreements, protecting workers' legal rights, processing grievances and labour disputes, and directly monitoring health and safety issues. The Act specified collective bargaining as a legitimate activity of trade unions.

7 The *Temporary Measures on Collective Wage Consultation* was implemented in 2000 and governed the principles and details of wage increases through collective consultation between the enterprise and the trade union/workers' representatives.

8 The *Provision Concerning the Administration of the Labour Market* was introduced in 2000, providing the basic principles that would underpin the emerging external labour market.

9 A new *Labour Contract Law* came into effect in 2008. The Act had gone through a series of modifications based on a large number of submissions received from the various parties. The objective of the law was to create a 'harmonious society' and to be more inclusive in its coverage. The Act requires employers to provide written contracts to all workers, restricts the use of temporary labour and makes it harder to lay off workers.

Clearly, the way human resources were managed and employment relations conducted were of growing concern to the government as they proceeded with their economic reforms. There was little doubt that the state saw people management as a major component of the economic restructuring and that a market economy could not be achieved without freeing up the employment system, supporting a strong external labour market and introducing a variety of legislative reforms to both protect the interests of workers and encourage investment by employers. The legislative and regulatory reforms over these three decades 'significantly influenced the relationship between enterprises and workers as well as affected the social and economic life of the society as a whole' (Zhu, Webber and Benson, 2010: 15).

Challenges of ongoing labour disputes and labour unrest

Since 2010, a number of ongoing problems and new issues have challenged employment relations at the macro level and labour management at the workplace. One of the most significant challenges is the ongoing labour unrest due to delays in wage payments, inadequate overtime payment and absence of social insurance contributions by employers. Another significant, although more recent, cause for labour unrest has been the industry policy changes and related structural reform which promotes advanced manu-facturing systems. This shift has led to the replacement of the traditional labour-intensive sectors resulting in the closure of aging factories and the redundancy of their workers (Tang, 2017). These labour conflicts are a direct challenge to the central government's goal of 'establishing a harmonious society'. Maintaining social stability (namely, *weiwen*, 'stability preserva-tion') has become the central focus and the major priority of national se-curity with the national budget for *weiwen* exceeding the national defence budget (Cooney, Biddulph and Zhu, 2013: 119). Thus, both the central government and local governments have treated labour unrest as the major obstacle for maintaining social stability. As a response, the central and provincial governments have developed new policy initiatives to ease the tensions and have managed any potential unrest by government intervention and legal mechanisms.

The various levels of government have adopted a top-down approach to manage the situation by proposing a comprehensive mechanism to achieve the so-called 'harmonizing labour relations' initially raised by the Vice Minister of Human Resource and Social Insurance in February 2013 (Wu, 2017). According to the Vice Minister's speech, the central government would work with provincial governments to identify a number of cities and districts that would serve as experimental zones in which a number of new initiatives would be implemented to ease the labour tensions by adopting new policies, linking different government agents, allocating new resources and improving the administrative methods and the quality of civil servants (Wu, 2017). One example of the implementation of this initiative is the nomination by the Guangdong provincial government, acting under the instruction of the central Ministry, of a number of cities and districts as the experimental zones, including the cities of Guangzhou, Shenzhen, Fushan and Huizhou, with a number of districts being involved, such as Huadu district in Guangzhou, Yantian district in Shenzhen, Shunde district in Fushan and Dayawan district in Huizhou. After the initial implementation, the central government passed a resolution in March 2015 on 'Establishing Harmonious Labour Relations' through the Central Party Committee and the State Council. This new policy required all levels of governments to pay particular attention to addressing labour issues with the goal of maintaining industrial harmony; officials' key performance indicators (KPIs) were directly linked with the overall performance of social stability in their related regions.

The overall objective of the central government is clear, namely, maintaining social harmony and stability. The detailed methods of dealing and managing potential labour tensions, however, rely on local governments at provincial and district levels to develop their own initiatives according to the particular situation in their region and their specific needs and challenges. By using Shenzhen city as an example, we can understand how the local government adopted certain policies and methods to deal with the particular challenges that existed in Shenzhen.

As one of the leading SEZs, Shenzhen undertook economic reform and opened up to foreign investment and international trade in the early 1980s (Zhu, 1995). As the leading SEZ in China, Shenzhen has been at the frontier in implementing many new policies, such as an 'experimental zone' to try out new policies and new ways of doing things. This reform approach has been described as 'crossing the river by feeling the stones' (Zhu, Webber and Benson, 2010). In recent years, Shenzhen has been faced with certain challenges which did not exist in the earlier years of reform. For example, the international economic tensions and related slowdown of the global economy have negatively influenced the overall industrial sectors in Shenzhen, given that the majority of the firms in Shenzhen rely on export markets. Consequently, the economic slowdown has negatively influenced the overall business operations of many firms due to accumulating debts, and together with the reduced cash flow has jeopardized business owners' ability to pay wages and overtime promptly. Some owners who could not make payments abandoned their businesses, causing many cases of severe labour unrest.

According to official records, between 2013 and 2015, the Shenzhen government's labour mediation and arbitration agents received 31,872, 39,047 and 31,471 labour disputes and unrest cases, respectively. Among them, the total number of cases that were processed through the arbitration courts were 27,507, 28,226 and 30,937 for these three years, respectively (Yang, B. H., 2017). These figures demonstrate that the majority of cases could not be solved by mediation and were referred to the arbitration courts. This was not the situation before 2010 when most disputes were solved through mediation (Zhu, Webber and Benson, 2010), which suggests that the seriousness of the confrontation between owners and workers regarding timely payment of wages and overtime has accelerated since 2010.

Governments' policy on preventing and handling labour disputes and unrest

Under the central government's policies, local governments have developed a number of policy initiatives to manage the labour dispute situation, preventing further labour unrest and achieving the goal of 'maintaining social harmony'. In Shenzhen, for example, the government established four policy initiatives with detailed implementing mechanisms:

1   Perfecting workers' wage payment guarantee mechanism

Under this policy initiative, the government undertook three actions. First, the government arranged regular inspection teams to visit companies and inspect their wage system and the record of wage payments. If companies were found to be not meeting the required standards, they would receive a warning and a fine. According to official records, in October 2015, when the government inspection teams carried out the so-called 'comprehensive inspection campaign' (*jiancha daxingdong*), some 15,526 companies were inspected covering 1.72 million employees (Yang, B. H., 2017).

Second, when the inspection teams found companies were not paying workers adequately and on time, they referred these cases to various government agencies, including the Office of Maintaining Stability (*weiwen ban*), Public Security, Department of Human Resources, Public Procuration and the People's Court. A cross-departmental committee was established to handle serious cases where owners refused to pay workers adequate compensation. For example, between 2013 and 2015, the committee handled over 300 serious cases and 189 business owners were arrested for criminal offences (Yang, B. H., 2017).

Third, the government passed a new regulation titled *Shenzhen SEZ Owed Wages Guaranteed Regulation* (Wu, 2017). The regulation specifies that each firm has to pay an annual wages guarantee fee of RMB 400 per employee. These fees are pooled and allow the local labour bureaus to establish a Wages Guaranteed Fund to support workers when their employers do not pay workers the required wages, or if employees do not receive compensation in cases where employers abandon their businesses. The local government can carry out legal action against these business owners as well as attempt to recover monies owed to the workers and the Wages Guaranteed Fund. Between 2013 and 2015, for example, the local Human Resources and Social Insurance Departments at the district level in Shenzhen paid out total owed wages of RMB 140 million covering 260,000 workers (Yang, B. H., 2017). This approach by the government has prevented many potential cases of labour unrest and has contributed to the maintenance of social harmony.

2 Improving labour relations through the labour contract system

One important labour protection mechanism is the use of individual and collective labour contracts to manage the relevant benefits, duties and responsibilities for both employees and employers. If a labour dispute occurs, the detailed contract provisions can provide the foundation for labour mediation and arbitration agents to determine the party at fault and the remedy. Hence, another important policy initiative has been the promotion of the labour contract system through education and campaigns at the firm level. According to official records (Yang, B. H., 2017), by the end of 2015, the individual labour contract coverage reached 94 per cent and collective contract coverage reached 82 per cent. At the same time, minimum wage standards were also established, increasing this wage from RMB 1100 per month in 2011 to RMB 2030 per month in 2015. By undertaking these actions, the various levels of government clearly wished to manage labour relations through a contractual or 'rule of law' approach underpinned by an effective labour mediation and arbitration system. In addition, the provision of minimum wage standards would protect workers' income levels and potentially avert further labour unrest.

3 Enforcement of labour regulations and the labour inspection mechanism

Many detailed labour regulations have been established within the labour dispute complaint system, dealing with collective or group-based industrial unrest (more than 30 employees involved) and labour standards inspection mechanisms, among others. However, the lack of regulation enforcement and related enforcement mechanisms is a widespread problem. In order to effectively implement new policies and enforce new regulations, the Shenzhen government has established a four-level network at the city, district, street and residential community levels. A 'labour situation information sharing platform' allows details regarding labour dispute complaints to be shared within the networks and handled by relevant government agents. A government inspection team is immediately appointed to collect evidence and hear representations from both sides. A mediation team is introduced to the parties to explore possible solutions and, if this is not successful, the case is then referred to the arbitration court. This 'one-line mechanism' moves from 'information sharing' to 'inspection' and then to 'mediation and arbitration', effectively handling any labour dispute case at the firm level and preventing it from becoming a 'social disturbing event' (Wu, 2017).

4 Reforming the labour dispute mediation and arbitration system The mediation and arbitration processes have become critical elements of the labour dispute resolution system. In general, the system has proved effective in handling labour disputes and preventing further escalation

of labour unrest. However, a number of problems existing within the system require the relevant levels of government to develop further initiatives and strategies. Such problems include the lack of capable mediation and arbitration personnel and the increasing volume of labour dispute cases, both of which have directly impacted on the length of time to process cases and to finalize the outcomes. Similarly, reducing paperwork by introducing an e-administration system may be a necessary step for improving the overall efficiency of the system. In addition, by providing an express channel for handling group-based disputes, with priority hearing and resolution processes, governments could also prevent the escalation of some serious labour unrest events.

Confronting new challenges of labour disputes and unrest

Despite the introduction of many new policy initiatives and regulations in recent years to address the challenging issues of labour disputes and unrest, new issues have arisen that challenge these developments. These challenges or issues include: 1) owners transferring money through different channels to avoid paying owed wages and/or making it more difficult to pay back workers quickly, 2) owners claiming bankruptcy to avoid paying wages owed and 3) company ownership changes and relocation of businesses to essentially avoid wage payments, which will negatively influence workers' well-being and almost certainly will generate new waves of labour unrest (Yang, B. H., 2017).

Dealing with these new challenges will require all levels of relevant government agencies to be vigilant and monitor potential crises, and to set up early warning systems to prevent new events of labour unrest. Improved coordination among different government agencies is also required to improve the effectiveness of the system. More personnel support in relevant areas by recruiting new staff members and providing more focused training is also required. Such actions could ease the imbalance between increasing demand for effective policy implementation and regulation enforcement and the excessive time taken to handle disputes due to the shortage of capable civil servants.

Shortages in labour supply

Another policy priority area is addressing the ongoing labour supply issues due to the demographic changes taking place (e.g. ageing population and declining birth rate) and other factors, such as regional competition for talent, increasing labour costs and the shifting industrial structure from labour-intensive to capital-intensive and high-tech manufacturing. In addition, nearly 50 per cent of new labour market entrants are graduates from vocational colleges and universities (Ni, 2017), who prefer to be located in the major urban and industrial centres. These factors result in an uneven supply of labour between different regions. The overall number of rural migrant workers has also been declining due to widespread industrialization across the entire country resulting in more work opportunities in their home towns and regions and less desire to migrate to large coastal cities (Tang, 2018). Pressure has increased on governments and business to shift the industry structure from labour-intensive work to more capital-intensive work through computerized machinery-based manufacturing production systems and high-tech and internet-based approaches (Research Group, 2018).

Consequently, the level of competition for labour has intensified in recent years, and local governments in different regions have offered incentives to attract workers, especially skilled workers. These incentives have included providing local *hukou* status, housing allowances and local schooling opportunities for their children (Tang, 2018). In addition, as the labour shortages have become more pronounced, local governments and business owners have increased wages through increases in the regional-based minimum wages set by local governments as well as nominal wages paid by employers (Zen, 2018). These developments will be discussed more fully in the following section.

In addressing the challenges of labour shortages and the increasing cost of production, in large part due to increases in labour costs, governments and business owners have moved the direction of industrial development towards more advanced manufacturing with computerized machinery, high-tech-oriented production and knowledge-based innovative industries (Tang, 2018). The central government has changed its industrial development slogan from 'Made in China' to 'Created in China', and local governments have also followed this shift by adopting the industrial policy of *tenglong huanniao* (empty the bird cage by getting rid of the old bird for the new bird to move in), which means removing the old industry and making space for the new advanced industry to move in (Min and Zhu, 2020). This has led to central and local governments adopting new policy incentives to promote an advanced manufacturing industry, such as replacing the business tax (sale tax) by a value added tax, reducing tax contribution to an average level of 6 per cent (Author's interview, 2019), and reducing company income tax from 25 per cent to 15 per cent for companies engaged in R&D and advanced manufacturing (Author's interview, 2019). Another initiative is lower interest rates on bank loans (e.g. 4–6 per cent interest rate compared with commercial loans at an average rate of 10 per cent) to support sizable advanced high-tech enterprises (Author's interview, 2019). Companies have also reduced labour demand and costs by introducing a greater degree of automation into their production processes. For example, Foxconn has reduced by more than 50 per cent its total number of employees and introduced more than 40,000 robots into its production sites nationwide (Ni, 2017). The efforts made by governments and business owners to cope with the challenges associated with labour supply have thus led to significant shifts in industry structure and employment with improved global competitiveness (Tang, 2018).

Balancing productivity and workers' well-being

A major challenge in undertaking reforms stemming from labour shortages and rising labour costs is maintaining a balance between improving productivity and workers' well-being; the latter primarily achieved through adjustments to wages. Since 2010, the wage gap has become wider between different industry sectors and different company sizes as well as between workers with different backgrounds (e.g. level of education, number of working years, position, qualifications and occupation).

Guangdong province, for instance, is a typical example given its location adjacent to Hong Kong, where there are more international connections and advanced industry sites. Hong Kong also has greater experience in managing change brought about by industrial restructuring from lower to advanced manufacturing processes and a shift from labour-intensive to more automation-oriented industry and a service-oriented economy. According to official data, among 18 industry sectors in Guangdong in 2016, the highest wages were in the financial sector with a monthly average wage of RMB 8,032, followed by the scientific and technological service sector with RMB 7,126 per month and the telecommunication, software and the IT service sector with RMB 6,452 per month (Zen, 2017). The lowest wage rates were in the hotel and restaurant sector with an average of RMB 3,113 per month, followed by the culture, sports and other entertainment sector with RMB 3,321 per month and the agribusiness sector with RMB 3,563 per month (Zen, 2017). The wage gap between highest and lowest sectors could thus reach almost RMB 5,000 per month or a factor of 2.6 times.

A number of organizational, demographic and personal factors also account for differences in wages or, more simply, the wage gap. Large companies normally pay higher wages compared with small and medium enterprises. For example, the average wages in 2016 were RMB 4,503 per month at large firms, RMB 4,019 per month at medium firms and RMB 3,408 per month at small firms (Zen, 2017). Differences between employees also accounted for some variation in wages. For instance, education was one of the important factors influencing wage levels. Employees with postgraduate degrees (i.e. Master's and PhD) had the highest average wage level at RMB 11,094 per month in comparison with employees with middle school education or below who only earned an average of RMB 3,199 per month (Zen, 2017).

Work experience or tenure is another important factor influencing wages. The above-mentioned official data indicated that this factor was most pronounced when combined with education. For example, employees with a postgraduate degree plus more than 11 years of work experience could earn more than RMB 16,600 per month compared with employees who had similar qualifications but had only worked for two to three years and could only earn around RMB 8,300 per month. In addition, employees with university degrees and more than 11 years of work experience earned RMB 9,880 per month compared with employees who had similar degrees but only worked for one year, earning RMB 4,705 per month (Zen, 2017). A similar situation also applied to employees with a high school or vocational school certificate as well as employees with middle school qualifications or below. For instance, employees who had a high school or vocational school qualification and more than 11 years of work experience earned RMB 4,270 per month compared with employees who had similar qualifications but had only worked for one year, earning RMB 3,150 per month. Similarly, for employees with middle school or a lower level of qualification, the difference was RMB 3,326 per month compared to RMB 3,011 per month, respectively (Zen, 2017).

Employees' positions within their organizations also explain part of the wage differences. For instance, employees who held managerial positions earned an average wage of RMB 5,290 per month compared with regular skilled workers who earned RMB 3,395 per month. This difference is further highlighted by considering the highest potential wage for these two groups: RMB 21,126 per month for managerial employees compared to RMB 8,402 per month for regular skilled workers (Zen, 2017). In the case of employees with professional qualifications and undertaking technical jobs, a senior professional employee earned an average wage of RMB 6,847 per month compared with employees who held a lower level of professional qualification and earned an average wage of RMB 4,626 per month. The highest wage for employees who held a senior professional qualification was RMB 24,451 per month compared to the top wage for employees with lower professional qualifications earning RMB 13,517 per month (Zen, 2017).

New economic sectors have also contributed to wage differences due to labour supply and demand issues, which have led to a rapid increase in wages. For example, over the period 2013–2016, sectors such as the telecommunication, software and IT sector enjoyed an annual increase in wages of 16.4 per cent per annum, the real estate sector saw wages grow by 25.7 per cent annually and wages in the scientific and technological service sector increased by 14.8 per cent per annum. However, the more traditional sectors, particularly the labour-intensive manufacturing industry, experienced very slow wage growth over this same period (Zen, 2017). The speed of economic development, labour supply and demand issues and the rapid growth of new economic sectors have collectively transformed the wage structure in China. This has led to questions being raised as to whether the new wage system maintains the distributive justice and fairness of the system it is replacing. If not, the potential for significant labour unrest will have increased.

Such concerns have led to a number of policy initiatives being implemented over the past decade, including:

1   Job creation for maintaining full employment (i.e. the overall national unemployment rate remains below 4 per cent) by focusing on assisting graduates to find employment. This includes detailed financial support for employers to train newly recruited graduates as well as financial incentives for graduates establishing start-up businesses.
2   Connecting different government agencies so as to support older, disabled and long-term unemployed people to undertake training and obtain new jobs.
3   Promoting entrepreneurship among domestic migrant workers and university graduates to develop new business in their home town with seed funds and low interest rate loans.
4   Using big data and cloud technology to promote information sharing regarding employment opportunities and labour supply issues among different regions and between urban and rural areas.
5   Implementing the 'Plan of Improving All Citizens' Skills' through the development of new economies and new high-tech industries. A new online training model, referred to as the 'internet + professional training', has been implemented with the purpose of matching skills with the needs of the developing new economies and advanced industrial sectors. This distance training and education is targeting workers located in remote rural regions.
6   Establishing a comprehensive data pool and information sharing platform nationwide to share and monitor the different conditions regarding wages and social insurances across the entire country. This move will allow governments and employers to make appropriate adjustments to their strategies in different regions. Employees will also be able to compare their own situation with their counterparts elsewhere and thus make decisions about staying in their present location or moving elsewhere to find better pay and conditions (Tang, 2017, 2018).

Through the linking of productivity improvements with wage increases and other job creation, information sharing and labour relations monitoring mechanisms, governments and business owners have benefited from a relatively sustainable economic growth with an improvement in the working life of employees. As a consequence, the tensions inherent in labour disputes and the maintenance of 'harmonious labour relations' appear to be manageable.

Managing social insurances

Providing adequate social insurance for workers has been a major objective under the economic reform policy. Since the Social Insurance Law was implemented in 2010 (Social Insurance Law, 2010), governments at all levels have made efforts to implement the law by developing a variety of enforcement mechanisms and monitoring systems. The law covers the five major social insurance types, namely, pensions, medical care, injury, unemployment and maternity provisions. In addition, in order to ease the difficulty in finding an apartment experienced by young workers, governments have developed policies on housing allowances as part of the overall benefit package for formally employed contract workers (China Briefing, 2019a). From this time, the so-called 'five insurances and one housing allowance' (*wuxian yijin*) has been the term referring to the major employment benefits in China. However, according to Cooney et al. (2013), the law might not cover many causal workers other than in relation to injury insurance. In addition, many financially struggling firms were unable to pay the full amount of social insurances on time and other firms attempted to avoid paying the housing allowance to workers who did not have local *hukou* status. This latter action tended to re-enforce the different treatment of workers based on the distinction between workers with a local *hukou* and others who are migrant workers (Cooney et al., 2013).

The role of governments in the process of implementing the Social Insurance Law has shifted from having an emphasis on compliance with the law through monitoring and inspection (i.e. from 2010 to 2015) to revising the requirements of the law in order to reduce the financial burden on firms (i.e. from 2016 to the present). One of the major obstacles to the full implementation of the law was the economic slowdown, with many employers complaining about the increased financial burden of fully complying with the law. For example, research shows that, on average, the total value of social insurance contributions was equivalent to an additional 45 per cent of the employee's wage. When the economic slowdown emerged in 2016, the situation deteriorated with many SMEs claiming bankruptcy. The central government was concerned with this development and the State Council responded by issuing a policy on reducing the financial burden on firms and modifying the required social insurance contributions from firms (Y. Zhang, 2019). For instance, in 2016, the Shenzhen government followed the central government instruction by reducing firms' social insurance contribution by 50 per cent in the areas of injury, unemployment and maternity coverage (Zen and Zhou, 2017). In order to demonstrate that the government supported firms' good behaviour, the Shenzhen government also provided financial subsidies to firms that fulfilled their required social insurance obligations as well as did not make workers redundant during economically difficult times. According to the official data, 70,983 firms were granted these financial subsidies in Shenzhen in 2016 (Zen and Zhou, 2017).

The implications for employers and employees

Over the last 10 years, numerous policies and regulations have been modified significantly to cope with the changes in the economic and political contexts both in China and internationally. During the earlier years of the last decade, the policy emphasis was on the protection of labour rights, such as developing the labour contract systems (i.e. both individual and collective), labour law enforcement through labour dispute inspection, mediation and arbitration, and promoting a wider coverage of various social insurances. In more recent years, the policy has emphasized a more balanced approach towards business survival and development on the one hand and workers' well-being on the other hand. As mentioned earlier in this chapter, this policy shift has been underpinned by the negative influence of the economic slowdown and industrial restructuring which has adopted more advanced technology and systems. In the following chapters, we will provide a more detailed analysis of employers' and employees' responses to policy and regulation changes; in this chapter, we provide some general observations to highlight the overall importance of these developments.

Employers have responded in various ways to these important policy and regulation shifts. In earlier years (i.e. 2010–2015), the major concerns of employers related to the increased costs associated with implementing the relevant policies and regulations, in particular, the costs related to the full implementation of the required five social insurances. For instance, the cost of creating one extra job that required the payment of an additional 45 per cent on top of the normal salary for social insurances was simply seen as too expensive for many business owners, particularly SME owners. This led to employers' associations at different levels lobbying governments to relax the relevant policies (China Briefing, 2019b). This action seemed to have an effect as in 2016 the governments modified the relevant policies and regulations by reducing the proportion of employers' social insurance contributions. Other important changes in this period included taxation reform where a valued added tax replaced the existing sales tax but at a lower rate, the reduction of company income tax, and direct financial support through lower interest loans, assisting many employers to continue their business operations. The increased labour costs, including rising salaries, coupled with labour shortages, have also led many employers to introduce new technology into their production processes as a way of making their business operations more viable (Tang, 2018). Overall, employers have expressed more positive responses towards the policy shift in recent years (Author's interview, 2019).

Employees have generally found it challenging to understand the relevant policies and regulations and to be aware of how to use these to protect their interests and rights (Cooney et al., 2013). Governments have attempted, at least in part, to rectify this situation. Over the past decade, the Human Resource and Social Insurance Department (i.e. formerly the Labour Bureau), in cooperation with the branches of trade unions at different levels, have developed various training programmes to inform employees about the relevant policies and regulations and how they can use them to protect their interests (Wang, 2017; Feng, 2017). The overall reaction of employees towards these policy changes has been mixed. Employees and their representatives have welcomed the implementation of the labour contracts system, the establishment of the minimum wage level, the Guarantee Wage

Fund for preventing wage arrears and the implementation of five social insurance coverages (Wu, 2017). Nevertheless, some employees may perceive such changes more negatively as they may receive different entitlements, benefits and treatment due to their different social and economic backgrounds. For example, migrant workers and causal workers have not received many of the benefits received by local and regular workers (Cooney, 2013; Ni, 2017).

The union branches have been engaged in a more institutionalized industrial relations environment through their involvement in the labour dispute mediation mechanisms at the firm level. These mechanisms include enterprise mediation committees as well as district- and city-level mediation committees attached to the Human Resource and Social Security Department. In Shenzhen, for example, under instruction from the city-level trade union authority, union branches at the district and firm levels can be actively involved in resolving labour disputes, particularly disputes that could involve industrial action (Wang, 2017; Feng, 2017). Clearly, by attempting to resolve disputes at the firm level, or district level for firms without union branches, could lead to agreement between unions and employers on the conditions necessary to resolve the underlying issues. In doing so, the government and trade unions could prevent the situation from leading to social unrest, thus maintaining the social harmony that is currently the most important policy priority for governments at all levels.

At the firm level, union branches have also been actively involved in establishing labour contract systems, particularly promoting collective contracts. For example, in 2016 over 84 per cent firms in Shenzhen signed a collective contract due to the unions' effort in promoting union branches at the firm level which enabled them to negotiate with employers and sign a collective contract (Liu and Chen, 2017).

Conclusion

As a transitional economy, China's economic policy in general, and policy reforms in employment relations and labour management systems in particular, have oscillated over the last decade. Many internal and external factors have influenced the policy shift, but the overarching goals of the state have been to develop a strong economy and a harmonious society. Such goals have been underpinned by the quest for improved competitiveness (i.e. through science and technology, advanced manufacturing systems and a highly skilled workforce), efficient management systems both in the public and private sectors and a better life for the majority of citizens (i.e. the creation of a strong and growing middle class) (Min and Zhu, 2020). These are key indicators of the so-called 'China Dreams' (Min and Zhu, 2020).

The reality, however, may be far from the ideal picture presented by the 'China Dreams'. Ongoing labour disputes and even regular labour unrest have challenged the notion of 'maintaining social harmony'. In order to prevent the further escalation of social unrest, the governments have used policy initiatives and regulations to maintain their control in a more in-stitutionalized manner, such as establishing the labour contract systems at the firm level, labour dispute mediation and arbitration systems, expanding the social insurance system and introducing minimum wage standards. By adopting a more balanced approach towards continued economic growth and attempting to meet the twin objectives of support for business as well as protecting workers' basic rights and well-being, governments hope to be able to manage the potential instability and unrest so as to continue with strong economic development. This is the path of economic reform in China in this decade, although it remains uncertain whether such an expectation is rea-listic. In exploring the realization of these objectives and expectations, the following chapters will undertake a firm-level analysis to understand how management and workers manage their daily work life and respond to daily challenges at the workplace.

3 Management initiatives on work and labour management

Introduction

In the previous chapter, we provided a detailed review of the recent macro-level changes over the past 10 years related to the key economic, legal and industrial policy reforms that have impacted business management in general and labour management in particular. Macro-economic reform, however, requires micro-economic initiatives and action on the part of enterprise managers and workers for such policy changes to be effective (Zhu, Webber and Benson, 2010). In this chapter, therefore, we focus on management's response to these reforms and the adoption of particular ways of labour management at the enterprise level.

In addressing these issues, we will utilize survey data collected among managers of 60 enterprises located in the north (i.e. Beijing and Hebei) and the south (i.e. Guangdong and Hunan). The chapter will commence with a discussion on managers' views on the influence of government policy on their enterprise, followed by a section that examines the recruitment of new types of employees, such as dispatched and non-local resident workers. We are particularly interested in the reasons for using such workers and whether these workers are treated the same as regular local employees. The next section focuses on employee pay, conditions of work and the opportunities for promotion and participation in management. We then turn our attention to the management of collective agreements and labour disputes, followed by a discussion on the problems and difficulties of managing different types of employees. The final substantial section of the chapter will explore the major management changes that have occurred over the past decade. In utilizing various examples from our survey interviews, we will label the particular company referred to according to the following convention: Beijing company 1 will be referred to as BJC1, Hebei company 1 as HBC1, Hunan company 1 as HNC1 and Guangdong company 1 as GDC1.

Influence of government policy on the enterprise

In the management survey, a number of questions addressed managers' views on the major impacts of government policy and labour regulations on their company, the way their company kept up to date with new government policy and labour regulations initiatives and the manner in which government ensured compliance with the new regulations.

Among the sample of managers, there were some common as well as varied responses. For example, the manager of BJC1 claimed: "Previously the government didn't pay any attention to implementing the regulations; now they often request various kinds of documents and are stricter on management and control." In order to keep abreast of the regulation changes, the company now "discusses legal issues concerning employment conditions and labour mobility with lawyers" and uses "internet information to update their knowledge of government regulations". According to this manager, the government's role in law enforcement has also been strengthened through "regular inspections by government agents".

Other managers, however, were more concerned about the negative aspects of the governments' role. For example, the manager of HNC1 felt that "some government policies have been arbitrarily promoted by the media as propaganda. Some policies have difficulties in implementation, such as work injuries. In most cases, the company has to take full responsibilities, but with little government support." In contrast, positive responses from managers included the claim made by the manager of HNC9 that "the government provides regular information on new labour laws and regulations. Based on that, our company provides training with detailed information. Given the awareness of the relevant regulations, employees will complain if things happen that are not consistent with the regulations. The government labour department will also conduct inspections. Labour supervision and inspection teams will sometimes come for an inspection as well."

From these responses, we can see an increasing effort made by governments (i.e. both the central and local governments) on implementation and enforcement of the new labour laws and regulations. Companies also take initiatives for providing relevant training and legal awareness among employees. Consequently, employees are more aware of their legal rights and obligations and act accordingly. At the same time, employers are also under greater obligation to follow various laws and are thus increasingly using legal means and lawyers to protect their interests. The overall trajectory is towards more institutionalized and 'rule of law' oriented labour management, though negative elements such as media propaganda and government inaction do exist in certain locations and in certain labour management areas, such as work-related injuries.

Recruitment of new types of employees

As discussed in Chapter 2, in recent years, due to the growing ageing population and competition for workers between firms and regions, the shortage of labour has become a serious problem for governments and firms (Flannery, 2020). In addressing this labour shortage, the recruitment of a new generation of employees (Zhu and Warner, 2018), particularly the recruitment of dispatched and non-local resident workers, has become a challenging issue for many companies in China. Generally speaking, dispatched workers are recruited by labour hire agents through a contract with an employer to supply labour and are sent to work at the workplace of that company. The individual labour contract is signed between workers and hiring agents. The company pays a lump sum service fee to the agent, including the wages and other benefits, which will be paid to these workers by the hiring agent (Cooney, Biddulph and Zhu, 2013). Non-local resident workers are workers who have labour contracts with companies but without local residential (*hukou*) status. As such, they can be seen as migrant workers but with an employment contract with the employer at that workplace.

In the management survey, we were interested in the reason for companies utilizing dispatched workers and non-local residents and whether these workers were treated the same as regular and local employees. We hoped this approach would allow us to understand the rationale for companies to employ such workers instead of regular contract workers and enter into such contracts, as well as whether the different types of workers were being treated equally and fairly.

Not all companies in China, however, use dispatched workers and/or non-local resident workers, as was the case with GDC4, a leading high-tech company. When GDC4 signed an individual labour contract, it offered the new employee assistance to obtain a local (Shenzhen SEZ) *hukou*, thus facilitating all its employees to become local residents. On the contrary, BJC1, for instance, did not use dispatched workers, but employed many non-local resident workers. The reason given was the "shortage of local skilled labour in Beijing". Other companies, such as BJC15, employed 8 per cent of its workforce as dispatched workers, but did not employ any non-local resident workers. In this case, the company claimed cost factors were important as it used "dispatched workers to fill the shortage of causal workers, as they are in junior positions with lower cost."

In recent years, there has been a general trend for more and more companies to utilize dispatched and non-local resident workers. The following managers' responses provide some of the rationale for doing so. For instance, BJC3 was a construction company that employed both dispatch workers and non-local resident workers. It employed 377 dispatched workers, which was 17 per cent of the total workforce. The reason given by the manager was that "construction companies always have large numbers of casual workers. We use dispatched workers to overcome the shortage of casual staff within the company with relatively less HR management effort; for example, we don't need to undertake recruitment and other HR related things." The company also employed 697 non-local resident workers, which amounted to 31 per cent of the company's total formal contract employees. This relatively high figure was "due to different construction sites in different locations. By using workers with different residential status, it was easier to arrange for workers to work on the sites near their home town."

The location of the enterprise or company is another element in using non-local resident workers. The manager of HBC2 stated that "we employ 39 per cent of our employees as non-local resident workers. There is no limitation on the residency requirement in our city. Shijiazhuang is not a big city like Beijing, residency is not restricted so we can employ as many non-local resident workers as we want." The manager of GDC1 gave a different reason for using non-local resident workers stating "our company employs more than 80 per cent non-local resident workers. The reason is because the local people are very rich and no longer want to work as factory workers. So, our 20 per cent local employees are mainly taking management or office work positions. As for the production workers, they are mainly migrant workers without local *hukou*."

Based on these representative responses, we can advance the following key conclusions:

1   The overall shortage of labour, particularly of skilled workers in major cities and industrial areas, drives the increase in the recruitment of dispatched workers and non-local resident workers.
2   Dispatched workers fill the gap created by the shortage of causal workers but with lower positions and wages.
3   Non-local resident workers also fill the gap created by labour shortages, but mainly in more highly skilled positions and at higher levels of wages.
4   Certain high-tech companies do not use dispatched workers due to their relatively lower skill levels and the companies are able to help their contract employees gain local *hukou* status with better work-life security and long-term commitment.
5   There were a variety of other reasons for using non-local labour, including using workers from nearby towns for project sites, and local people not being willing to take on labouring work due to the availability of more suitable jobs.

The above-mentioned peripheral forms of employment raise the question of whether these new types of workers are treated the same as the more formal and regular local workforce. In our management survey, we specifically asked about the components of income for the different types of employees, whether these employees were paid differently, whether overtime work was paid to all types of employees, whether the five insurances and the housing allowance was paid by the company to all employees and whether other benefits were provided to all employees.

BJC3, a northern-based company, provides a good example to begin this discussion as it employs both dispatched and non-local resident workers. The basic wage for all employees was the same and currently represents 70 per cent of the total wage package. Dispatched workers, however, earned only 10 per cent incentive pay compared to other types of employees who earn 20 per cent. All employees received another 10 per cent in benefits (e.g. subsidized meals). The remaining 10 per cent for dispatched workers was paid as a service fee to the hiring agent, which was deducted from the total wages of these workers. The response from the manager was that "there is no difference between non-local resident workers and local regular workers in terms of pay, but dispatched workers get less income." In this company, the monthly income of dispatched workers was around RMB 4,300 in comparison to RMB 5,100 for other regular local and non-local resident workers, RMB 4,500 for office workers and RMB 9,100 for senior managers. For overtime work pay, all the employees were paid similar rates and all types of employees received the five insurances and one housing allowance paid by the company.

Similarly, GDC1, a southern-based company, had some commonalities with BJC3 but also some important differences. Dispatched workers made up 7 per cent of employees in GDC1, whilst non-local resident workers made up nearly 80 per cent of all its workers. The proportion of total income, which was divided between basic wages, incentive pay, overtime pay and other benefits, were similar among the different types of employees. Total income, however, revealed a much wider variation. For example, manual workers earned a monthly income of about RMB 3,000 with no difference between dispatched, non-resident and local regular workers; however, others, such as office workers, could earn around RMB 8,000, R&D employees could earn between RMB 17,000 and RMB 67,000, and salespeople and senior managers could earn between RMB 17,000 and RMB 125,000. Dispatched workers were eligible for social insurance and housing allowance only after working for more than 6 months for the company. If the dispatched workers left earlier, no such payments were provided.

These two examples demonstrate some locational differences regarding the income level among different types of employees. Generally speaking, dispatched workers were at the lower end of the scale in terms of total income and other benefits, including social insurance coverage. Few differences are evident between non-local resident workers and local regular workers as long as they are all regular contract employees. However, the total income gap among different types of employees is much wider in the south than in the north. As such, companies operating in the north of China (e.g. Beijing) can be seen as relatively more egalitarian than companies in the southern regions (e.g. Guangdong).

Pay, conditions of work and other benefits

In order to understand the impact of reform on the management of pay, conditions of work and other benefits, we focus on the overall reward system, particularly on performance-based pay, working time, social insurance and other welfare benefits, as well as the opportunities for promotion and participation in management among different types of employees.

The general pay system is often referred to as the 'comprehensive pay system' with different components or proportions making up total income, but with a focus on performance outcomes. This has led to a combination package for most employees, including basic wages, skill and position wages, overtime pay, bonus for performance, allowances and other benefits. As such, the pay structure or packages have become quite diverse among different types of employees, but with a common focus on linking pay with performance. For example, senior managers generally receive basic wages, plus an annualized component and performance bonus. This offer is different from the package for production line workers, where piece rates and/ or an hourly rate plus a position/occupation rate and allowances for other benefits is common. In turn, this is different for sales/marketing employees, where basic wages plus sales commissions or bonuses generally represent a typical package.

The manager of BJC3, a state-owned construction and project management company, explained the wage system in his company as having a "different pay structure between ordinary employees and senior managers. Ordinary employees are paid 70 per cent as a basic wage, 20 per cent bonus and 10 per cent other benefits (e.g. dining and transport subsidies), whilst senior managers are paid 50 per cent basic wage and 50 per cent annual position salary linked to performance." In contrast, the manager of HNC1, a state-owned property management company, outlined a different arrangement where "everyone (including the managers) are paid a similar wage package, with a 90 per cent basic wage, 0.5 per cent overtime pay, 8 per cent bonuses and 1.5 per cent other benefits."

GDC1, a privately owned manufacturing firm, represents a different example. The manager provided a detailed description of the pay packages among different employees where the company has "different pay for people working in different jobs in order to reflect the overall company performance. Production workers are paid an 80 per cent basic wage, 10 per cent overtime pay, 5 per cent bonus and 5 per cent other benefits; technicians are paid a 70 per cent basic wage, 20 per cent bonus and 10 per cent other benefits; administrative employees are paid an 80 per cent basic wage and 20 per cent bonus, whilst sales employees and senior managers are paid a 50 per cent basic wages and a 50 per cent performance-based incentive."

Structurally, similar pay packages were also adopted by many Foreign invested enterprises (FIEs), such as GDC5, an investment company from the US. In this case, the manager explained that "as a foreign company, we pay attention to individual performance. Therefore, our pay packages also reflect this principle. For example, the production workers are paid a 75 per cent basic wage, a 21 per cent bonus and 4 per cent for other benefits; the sales employees are paid a 50 per cent basic wage, a 46 per cent bonus and 4 per cent for other benefits; administrative employees are paid an 84 per cent basic wage, a 14.2 per cent bonus and 1.80 per cent for other benefits, whilst senior managers are paid a 70 per cent basic wage, a 5 per cent position wage, a 10 per cent bonus and a 15 per cent annual salary component."

Analyzing the different pay packages adopted by companies, there appears to be a general division in pay systems among firms of different ownership structures. State-owned enterprises (SOEs) appear to have adopted a more traditionally oriented pay structure with similar packages for all employees as well as providing a higher proportion for basic wages and a lower proportion for incentive pay. It should be noted, however, that some SOEs have changed their pay structures in recent years with a greater emphasis on linking pay to performance. In contrast, privately owned firms, particularly FIEs, place more emphasis on performance, especially for sales employees and senior managers.

Do similar divisions also exist in the implementation of working conditions? To explore these conditions, we asked managers about working time, social insurance, welfare and other benefits. In terms of working time, we wanted to know the normal working time arrangements operating in the company (including normal weekly hours and overtime hours per week) among the different types of employees and whether the company had made any changes in the last five years.

The majority of companies adopted the statutory 8 hours per day and 40 hours per week working time arrangement. As the manager of HNC1 explained, "Most employees in our company have similar normal working time arrangements, namely, 8 hours per day and 40 hours per week. But we have different arrangements on overtime work, where frontline operation employees have between 8 and 32 hours per week, and administrative employees have 8 hours per week only." GDC3 adopted a different working time arrangement, referred to by the manager as the "comprehensive working time arrangement". This company manages large exhibition events, which is a cyclical activity with a peak season and a low season as demonstrated by the number of exhibitions each month. As a consequence, during the peak season, employees work long hours and the overtime hours (i.e. beyond 8 hours per day and 40 hours per week) are recorded with compensation being made as paid holidays during the low season. In contrast, the manager of GDC5 stated that employees follow a normal working pattern of 8 hours per day and 40 hours per week without any overtime work.

Most companies covered the five social insurances and provided a housing allowance for their employees (for details on the five insurances, see Chapter 2; Yang, G., 2017). A small number of companies, however, did not provide all the five insurances and/or did not provide the housing allowance for non-local residents or dispatched workers. For example, GDC1 covered the five insurances and housing allowance for regular contract workers, but not for dispatched workers. GDC7 covered only partially non-resident workers claiming that "employees who do not have a Shenzhen *hukou* are not entitled to unemployment insurance and maternity insurance." Clearly, disparities in employment conditions exist and such discrimination is primarily directed towards dispatched workers and employees who are non-local resident workers.

Another important aspect of employment is the opportunities for promotion and participation in management among different types of employees. In our survey, we asked managers about the criteria for promotion in their company, whether this has changed in the past five years, and whether their company had instituted some form of employee participation policy/scheme. It was clear that different promotion criteria had been adopted among the companies interviewed. BJC1, for example, identified only four areas as important five years ago for promotion, namely, "qualifications, skill/knowledge, hardworking and seniority". However, at the time of the research, these criteria had expanded considerably and the criterion 'hardworking' had been removed with "experience, attitude/personality, networks, loyalty/commitment and foreign language capacity" being added to the remaining three promotion criteria. In contrast, HNC1 had not changed its promotion criteria in the last five years, with the key criteria for promotion being "experience, attitude/personality, skill/knowledge, networks and loyalty/commitment". GDC9, on the other hand, had identified the simple combination of "skill/knowledge, loyalty/commitment and seniority" as the important criteria for promotion. These different responses demonstrate areas of importance for the individual companies. There appears to be a general division between companies that focus on the background of the employee (e.g. qualifications, experience and seniority) and companies more interested in behavioural-oriented elements such as attitude/personality and loyalty/commitment. It is interesting to note that 'hardworking' now has little relevance to promotion in modern China.

Employee participation through various means has been a hallmark of socialist China. Since the commencement of the reform agenda, and particularly over the past decade or so, enterprises have varied considerably in the way workers can be involved in decisions affecting their working life. Some enterprises have few avenues for workers to express their voice. For example, the manager of HBC3 acknowledged that his company had only instituted "regular formal meetings between manager/supervisor and employees". In contrast, the manager of GDC5 listed a number of policy initiatives, including "involvement schemes, information sharing, individual grievance system, surveys of employees' views about policy, suggestion schemes and regular formal meetings between manager/supervisor and employees". The company also had implemented "employee stock ownership and profit sharing" schemes. Not all the companies surveyed had adopted such a comprehensive set of employee participation practices. The majority of companies focused on only a limited number of the possibilities mentioned above; for example, BJC3 had implemented a degree of information sharing, formal performance evaluation meeting with managers, and an individual grievance system and suggestion scheme.

The overall state of company-based participation schemes appears to be determined, to a large extent, by location and enterprise ownership. Companies located in more opened economic regions, such as the southern region of Guangdong, are more likely to have implemented a variety of employee participation schemes compared to companies located in the north and inland regions. Moreover, FIE companies such as GDC5 have adopted international strategic HR practices, such as employee participation schemes, in contrast to indigenous companies, either SOEs (e.g. BJC3) or Domestic private enterprises (DPEs; e.g. HBC3).

Collective agreements and labour disputes

As discussed in Chapter 2, the management of collective agreements and labour disputes has been one of the most significant challenges facing company management and trade union branches at the enterprise level. At the macro level, the appropriate new legislation has been enacted, such as the new Labour Contract Law, amendments to the Trade Union Law, and revised labour dispute mediation and arbitration regulations. How have these macro polices impacted enterprises? We asked managers whether there was a collective agreement in the company and whether there had been any labour disputes within the company in the last five years.

Most companies surveyed had instituted collective contracts as legally required by the Labour Contract Law. There were, however, a number of companies that did not have a collective employment contract, such as HBC5, a small private trading firm with 54 employees. Some FIEs also did not have a collective contract, such as GDC5, which did not have a union to demand and monitor such a statutory requirement. Similarly, BJC1, a large private firm, did not have a collective contract since, as the manager explained, no union had been present in the firm. Some FIEs did, however, have a collective contract. For example, GDC3, a Japanese-owned company, has had a collective contract since 2011 which was signed between management and the local trade union branch. SOEs or firms that either grew out of SOEs or were joint venture (JV) partners generally had a trade union and also had collective contracts. For example, BJC3, an SOE, has had a collective contract since 1996 which had been, and continues to be, negotiated between the local union branch and the management. Another SOE, HNC1, also indicated they have had a collective contract since 2012 which had been facilitated by the union and signed with management.

An examination of labour disputes revealed that managers were confronted with a wide variety of problems. The manager of BJC1 revealed problems quite common in the construction industry when he explained that "the sub-contractor and investors did not pay on time, which left migrant workers fighting for money. The project had a net loss and so could not pay for wages. Employees also left the project, which caused problems remaining in the project, but our company was required to take the responsibility.

We have had many of these kinds of problems to deal with in the past five years." The manager conceded that the matter was finally resolved through mediation and only after the intervention of government.

Other problems confronting management related to employees breaking company policy. As the manager of GDC7 recalled, "Some employees did not follow the rules, but when we fine them, they did not agree with the punishment, and this led to disputes. Eventually, we solved the problems via the government labour arbitration court." The manager of BJC3 also provided a similar example claiming, "Some people violate company policies or they are not qualified for the relevant job. After being dismissed, some of them refused to follow the relevant procedures and sued the company in the labour arbitration court. We have to deal with those kinds of problems regularly." Other disputes were related to workers' injury and compensation. The manager of GDC1 pointed out that "every year, several work-related accidents would happen, and these would lead to workers' injuries and compensation disputes. These problems were not frequent and the company complied with the law to manage these with the help of a local labour agent."

Based on these examples, we can see the major barrier to having a collective contract is the lack of a union at the enterprise level. Within the group of enterprises making up this study, there are examples of both large and small DPEs and FIEs without a local union branch and thus, in most cases, no collective contract. According to the Trade Unions Law and Labour Contract Law, firms with more than 25 employees should set up an enterprise union and it is the obligation of both management and union to negotiate a collective contract (Wrest, 2017). Clearly, law enforcement remains a challenging issue in China and a number of the surveyed enterprises could face increased scrutiny by the authorities in the coming years. The majority of firms in this study, however, have established a collective contract with union involvement at the firm level. In addition, as we discussed in Chapter 2, managing labour disputes and maintaining social harmony have been the government's priority and the surveyed firms ensured that they addressed such issues through the legal process with the involvement of the local labour bureau mediation and arbitration system. The overall trend in the resolution of industrial disputes in recent years appears to have been the utilization of industrial relations institutions and legal processes.

Management of different types of employees

Although having different types of employees may have some advantages for firms, this diversity within an enterprise can lead to some problems and difficulties for management. By exploring this issue, we hope to develop an understanding of the current challenges facing management given the increasing diversity among the various types of employees. In our survey, we thus asked managers whether they had experienced any problems and difficulties regarding the performance of different type of employees, and, if so, what were these problems. In addition, we asked these managers to comment on each type of employee as well as the changes that have occurred in the last five years.

The manager of HNC6, a private construction company, highlighted the problem of managing dispatched workers and the company's relationship with the hiring agent given the lack of funding from its investor. In this case, "the investor did not provide sufficient funds regularly, and so we could not pay wages on time. We could not collect any management fees regarding the employment of dispatched workers and pay it to the hiring agent. Then the local Labour Bureau deducted our deposit from the Wage Protection Fund in order to protect the dispatched workers, and the money has been deducted regularly." The manager was also concerned about the company's own contract workers being "not very efficient" and the technicians' "lack of professional certificates and so could not attract big projects".

In contrast, the manager of GDC9, an FIE, complained about the administrative and management employees as "our administrative staff have a high turnover rate due to work pressure, and they are not comfortable with the job." Similarly, "the management team's lack of communication between departments creates serious conflicts." Another FIE, GDC5, suffered from a high turnover rate among its salespeople, causing the manager to complain that "those capable salespeople can easily leave the company and get another higher paid job in another company. We face an unstable workforce and some of our marketing strategies have to be reduced in certain ways to cope with this challenge." Another private company, BJC1, also raised the concern of the "high turnover rate among all the employees, including both local and non-local contract workers as well as administrative, sales and management staff. The competition for high quality workers has intensified in the last five years, particularly in a big city like Beijing."

From these responses, it can be seen that the major problems of managing different types of employees are associated with the overall labour management problems in China, namely, insufficient funding to pay workers adequately and on time, the labour shortages escalating the competition for qualified and skilled workers, and the high turnover among employees who can easily find a better job with better pay elsewhere. As we discussed in Chapter 2, the shortage of appropriate labour, competition for talented workers and increasing wages have placed many enterprises under pressure and represent a major challenge facing management in China in recent years.

Major management changes

In our research, we also wanted to explore major changes facing management in the past five years. We thus asked a number of questions, including whether management had adopted modern management systems in their company, whether changes had been made to management systems in the last five years, how employees had reacted to these changes and whether the firm had measured the effectiveness of such reforms.

The term 'modern management systems' refers to an important management reform agenda promoted by the Chinese government for improving the efficiency among SOEs and DPEs. A number of elements were seen as making up such a system, including a contemporary corporate governance system, a market-oriented organizational structure, a professional business management approach, a performance/incentive-based system, a comprehensive shareholding system and a corporate social responsibility (CSR) arrangement. The adoption of international standards, ISO 9000 and ISO 14000, was also considered important for firms to gain international recognition of business contracts and sub-contract arrangements with MNCs (Sardana and Zhu, 2017).

Our questions about the adoption of modern management systems led many managers to provide various examples to highlight their attitudes towards management changes. For example, the manager at HBC3, a small private trade company, defended the lack of change by declaring that "we are a sales company, not a manufacturing company. Our scale is very small; therefore, these key modern management items have not been adopted." In contrast, the manager at HNC6, a large private construction company, highlighted that the company "has adopted a modern corporate governance system, a market-oriented organizational structure, professional business management, a modern performance/incentive-based system, a comprehensive shareholding system and a corporate social responsibility (CSR) system." Considering the major changes in the last five years, he replied that "compared to five years ago, the position and occupation-related responsibility have been strengthened, especially on safety management." This manager felt that the company's employees supported these management initiatives, although he conceded that the company did not measure the effectiveness of such changes.

Among the SOEs, such as BJC3, the manager responded by stating that "the company has implemented the following systems, including a modern governance system, a market-oriented organizational structure, a professional management system, and ISO 9000 and ISO 14000." To facilitate such change, the "management structure has changed from the original three levels of management to the present two levels of management." As for the employees' response to these changes, he replied that the "reduced length of the management chain was better for the company's long-term development." To measure the effectiveness of this management reform, the company was "conducting a company-wide survey and calls democratic meetings to evaluate the outcomes."

Foreign companies also responded in a similar fashion to their domestic counterparts. GDC9, for example, had implemented many of the usual modern management systems, including modern corporate governance, a market-oriented organizational structure, professional management, modern performance/incentive-based management, a comprehensive shareholding system and a CSR scheme. In addition, these companies had adopted the international quality management standards of ISO 9000 and ISO 14000. Some major changes had occurred in the last five years, including "the company hired professional consultants to redesign the workflow and make the work process more efficient with less cost." The manager of GDC10 also presented a similar case, but emphasized employees' input as being critical to the reform process with the "company taking more employee opinions into consideration" and "using the employee survey as an instrument to collect feedback and improve the next round of reform."

The adoption of 'modern management systems' and international quality management standards such as ISO 9000 and ISO 14000 was clearly linked to the attempt by firms to increase the firms' competitiveness and international expansion. Clearly, FIEs bring many of the 'international best management practices' into China as part of their normal expansion to other countries and are often driven by home country management. For many indigenous companies, particularly SOEs and large DPEs, the adoption of such practices is not comprehensive nor their introduction systematically planned. The measures tend to be adopted on a piecemeal basis depending on the companies' needs and without much consideration of the supporting nature of 'bundles' of practices. Given the limited awareness and knowledge of such practices in small-sized DPEs, the financial cost of implementation and the varied capability of the owners, the adoption and integration of modern management elements into what may be a reasonably successful company at any one point in time seems less relevant to the companies' operations.

Conclusion

In order to analyze the impact of macro-economic policy at the enterprise level, this chapter focused on the micro-economic initiatives and actions on the part of managers. Based on our survey data collected from managers of 60 enterprises, we explored the different responses of enterprises to government policy initiatives, the recruitment of new types of employees, the management of pay and conditions of work, collective agreements and labour disputes, the challenges of managing different types of employees, and major management changes. These themes and some representative managers' responses are presented in Table 3.1.

There appears to be an increasing effort by governments at all levels (i.e. both central and local governments) to effectively implement and enforce new labour laws and regulations. In turn, companies are increasingly taking the initiative in providing training and improving legal awareness among employees. Consequently, employees are more aware of their statutory rights and obligations and are thus more likely to act accordingly.

Table 3.1 Managers' responses to labour management reform in China

Themes	Key management responses
The influence of government policy	1 *The major influences of government policy and labour regulations* "Previously the government didn't pay any attention to implementing the regulations, now they often request us to submit different kinds of documents, becoming stricter on management and control". "Some government policies have been arbitrarily promoted by the media as propaganda. Some policies have difficulties in implementation". 2 *Keeping up to date with new government policies and labour regulations* "The company discussed legal issues about employment conditions and labour mobility with lawyers" and using "internet information to update government regulations". "The government provides regular information on new labour laws and regulations. Based on that, our company provides training with detailed information". 3 *The government's effort to ensure compliance with labour regulations* "Regular inspections by the government agents".
Recruitment of new types of employees	1 *Companies' reasons for using dispatched workers and non-local residents* "Shortage of local skilled workforce". "Dispatched workers fill the shortage in the causal workforce, they are at junior positions with lower cost". "At different construction sites in different locations, we use workers with different residential status". "Company employs are more than 80 per cent non-local resident workers because the local people are very rich and no longer want to work as factory workers". 2 *Whether there is equal treatment compared with regular and local employees* "Dispatched workers are at the bottom in terms of total income and other benefits, including the social insurance coverage". "No differences between non-local resident workers and local regular workers as long as they are all formal contract employees". "Total income gap among different types of employees is much wider in the south than the north".

Themes	*Key management responses*
Management of pay and conditions of work	**1 Management of pay systems** "A general division is related to different ownership of firms". "SOEs have adopted a more traditionally oriented pay package: higher proportion on basic wage and less proportion on incentive pay". "In contrast, privately owned firms, particularly foreign-owned firms, put more weight on performance, especially for sales employees and senior managers". **2 Management of conditions of work** "The majority of companies adopted 8 hours per day and 40 hours per week working time arrangements". "Different arrangement on overtime work": 8–32 hours per week or seasonal (rotating work and paid holiday between peak and low seasons). **3 Social insurance and other welfare benefits** "The majority of companies covered the five social insurances and one housing allowance for their employees". "Disparity does exist among different companies and discrimination towards dispatched workers and non-local resident workers is reflected in the areas of social insurances and other welfare benefits". **4 Opportunities for promotion and participation in management** "Different companies emphasize different criteria, either with more background orientation or with more behaviourally oriented elements". "Being hard working is no longer important for promotion". "Companies located in more opened economic regions could adopt more employee-participation management systems. In addition, foreign-owned companies adopt more internationalized HR practices with emphasis on employee participation".
Management of collective agreements and labour disputes	**1 Collective agreements** "The majority of companies have established collective agreement". "A major barrier leading to not having a collective contract is the lack of union establishment at firm level".

(*Continued*)

Table 3.1 (Continued)

Themes	Key management responses
	"Law enforcement is still a challenging issue in China".
	2 *Managing labour disputes* "Companies pay attention to addressing these issues through the legal process with the involvement of local labour bureau mediation and arbitration systems".
The challenges of managing different types of employees	"Major problems of managing different types of employees are associated with overall labour management problems in China". "The key problems are still associated with paying workers adequately and on time". "Labour shortages caused escalation of competition for the qualified and skilled workforce, and consequently high turnover rates among staff members who could easily find a better job with better pay".
Major management changes	"In order to increase firms' competitiveness and international expansion, many companies have adopted 'modern management systems' and international quality standards such as ISO 9000 and ISO 14000". "FIEs bring many of the so-called 'international best practices' of management systems into China". "In SOEs and large DPEs, the adoption is not comprehensive, but selective, depending on the company's needs". "Small sized DPEs are still reluctant to adopt modern management systems and elements".

Source: Management survey.

Companies are more aware of their legal obligations and are increasingly utilizing the law and the services of lawyers to protect their interests. The overall trajectory is clearly towards more institutionalized mechanisms and the 'rule of law' oriented labour management approaches.

However, due to the overall shortages of labour, the trend is towards recruiting dispatched workers to fill the demand for causal workers, most of whom are in lower positions with commensurate lower wages. A similar trend can be seen in the use of non-local resident workers to fill the shortages in more skilled positions with a commensurate higher level of wages. In addition, our research highlights some important locational differences (i.e. south versus north), particularly concerning the income level among different types of employees, and dispatched workers in particular. This latter group of workers receives the lowest total of income and other employment benefits, including social insurance coverage.

The overall reward system appears to be differentiated by enterprise ownership, where SOEs have adopted a more traditionally oriented pay package in comparison with privately owned firms, particularly FIEs who put more weight on employee performance. Other working conditions, such as normal working hours, have been standardized across China since the implementation of the new Labour Contract Law, which specifies a standard 8 hours per day and 40 hours per week. Notwithstanding, overtime work and pay varies significantly between different types of firms. Most companies provide the five social insurances and one housing allowance for most of their employees, but disparities exist and discrimination towards dispatched and non-local resident workers is the reality in modern China. Opportunities for promotion are available, but this is somewhat unclear as there is no generally accepted set of criteria for promotion. What could be ascertained in our study was that companies primarily focused on either background criteria or behavioural-oriented characteristics, but usually not both. Employee participation in management did occur, but this again varied by location and ownership. Companies located in the more southern, open economic regions (i.e. Guangdong) appeared to adopt more employee-participation management systems in comparison with the companies located in the north and inland regions. Such practices were also more prevalent in FIEs due to the likelihood of importation of international HR best practices.

Most companies had established a collective employment contract, although smaller, domestic firms often disregarded this aspect of the revised labour laws mainly due to the lack of a union at the enterprise level. Once again, this finding demonstrates that law enforcement is still a challenging issue in modern China. In addition, as we discussed in Chapter 2, managing labour disputes and maintaining social harmony have been a major government priority for achieving social stability. From our research, it appears that firms addressed such issues through legal processes, particularly through the involvement of local labour bureau mediation and arbitration services. Although this finding demonstrates an institutionalizing of industrial relations in recent years, it does clash with the actions of smaller firms in their unwillingness to accept enterprise unionism.

Finally, our research demonstrates that the major problems of managing different types of employees are associated with the wider labour management problems in China, including the shortage of various types of labour, intense competition for highly qualified workers and rapidly increasing wages. These challenges have led firms to adopt 'modern management systems' and international quality management standards in order to improve firms' competitiveness and international expansion as well as attempting to maintain 'social harmony'. As pointed out throughout the chapter, the degree of enterprise reform varied by different ownership types and firm locations. The overall trajectory, however, appears to be towards more institutionalized, more modernized and more internationalized systems and practices. With these concluding remarks, we now proceed to Chapter 4, in which we turn to the impact of the macro-economic reform agenda on employees; namely, the responses of employees towards the policy influences and changes of management systems and practices.

4 Employees' experiences and responses to labour management reform

Introduction

Macro-economic reform in general and government policy and legislation on labour management in particular have been discussed in Chapters 1 and 2. In order to understand what impact these policy initiatives and legislation have had at the firm level, we provided an analysis of the micro-economic initiatives and responses of enterprise managers in Chapter 3. In the present chapter, we extend that analysis to discuss the impact of the macro-economic reform agenda on employees; more specifically, the responses of employees to policy influences and changes in management systems and practices. As shown in a previous work, such reform can have a significant impact on employees' working life (Zhu, Webber and Benson, 2010).

This chapter will address five key themes in exploring employees' experiences of, and responses to, labour management reform. The first theme relates to the key changes to labour management in the company, emanating from the macro-economic reform, which have impacted on employees. Secondly, we address the main changes to pay, working time (including overtime) and other benefits which, for most individual workers, represent the critical aspects of enterprise reform. The third theme relates to the changes to employment contracts and the resultant types of employment, while the fourth relates to career development and, in particular, how reform has impacted on this development, training and promotion. Finally, the fifth theme elucidates us on the manner in which relationships with management have developed post enterprise reform and the way workers are able to best communicate with their supervisors.

As in the previous chapter, in addressing these themes we have utilized qualitative research data, although in this case from the employee survey, so as to illustrate how workers feel about change and how they have individually responded. In order to match the data using the convention introduced in Chapter 3, we will identify workers within their particular company using the following format: Beijing company 1 will be referred to as BJC1, Hebei company 1 as HBC1, Hunan company 1 as HNC1, and Guangdong company 1 as GDC1. Likewise, the analysis will be broken down according to the enterprise location, namely, the north (Beijing and Hebei) and the south (Hunan and Guangdong), and different enterprise ownership structures, namely, State-owned enterprises (SOEs), Joint stock companies (JSCs), Domestic private enterprises (DPEs) and Joint venture (JV)/Foreign invested enterprises (FIEs). Where relevant, however, we also consider some key employee characteristics, such as employment type (regular contract vs. dispatched workers), professional certification or qualifications, and residence status. By doing so, we can probe a little deeper into the different impacts and responses of employees from different locations and firms and understand what kind of disparities exist in various types of workplaces.

Economic reform and key changes to labour management

As discussed in earlier chapters, the major policy changes during the recent period of economic reform have had a significant influence on management policy and practices at the enterprise or the firm level (see also Min, Bambacas and Zhu, 2017). The key objective underpinning these changes is related to improving the overall productivity and efficiency of enterprises, as well as ensuring workers receive appropriate wages, social insurance and other benefits in line with the new labour laws, and statutory provisions and regulations (ICLG, 2020). It is, however, unclear how workers have been affected and have responded to these changes. In an attempt to shed more light on this perspective, we asked workers participating in the survey to identify the one key change in terms of organization of work in the last five years and explain how this change had affected their working life, what other change they would like to see and how they would achieve this change.

Among the respondents, workers responded quite differently depending on their backgrounds. There was, however, a clear division between dispatched workers and regular contract workers (including both local and non-local resident contract workers). Given that work conditions were arranged by labour hire agents, dispatched workers were generally under fixed contract with those agents, and thus many of these workers experienced little change. In contrast, contract workers, including local and non-local residents, experienced significant changes at their workplace. Such differences become clear when comparing and contrasting the different responses and breaking these down according to the two regions and different ownership structures.

In the north (Beijing and Hebei), many employees, for example, in BJC3, an SOE, identified a number of changes, including reduced overtime work due to the enterprise complying with the enforcement of new labour regulations on overtime work, more performance-based evaluation with KPI assessment, annual wage increases (although typically accompanied by increased workloads), increases in social insurance coverage and improved other benefits. People with professional roles (e.g. technicians and team leaders) also indicated there was more HR career planning with promotion opportunities. Similarly, employees of BJC8, a JSC, claimed more positive changes, including adjustment in working hours, reduced working time, promotion, less overtime work and greater wage increases.

This improvement was not always the case. Employees of a DPE in Hebei (HBC4) reported: "More overtime work and more pressure on performing well with possible deduction of bonus and other benefits if we don't perform well". The change to a more performance-based assessment was also seen as a negative outcome of the reform process by many workers, in both SOEs and DPEs, who felt anxious about the pressure created in attempting to balance increased workloads and performing well. Other workers claimed this change required employees to learn new skills in order to perform well. Other changes, such as increased wages, improved welfare provisions and career planning initiatives, were, as was expected, perceived as welcomed changes.

In contrast, many employees in the south (Guangdong and Hunan) identified a deterioration in working conditions. Workers in a number of companies (GDC1, GDC3, GCD7, HNC6 and HNC12) mentioned "more overtime work" (e.g. increased 25 per cent on average) and "more efficiency-oriented management systems, and higher end year incentive bonus but with an increased workload". Similar to workers in the north, those in the south pointed out increased promotion opportunities for employees with professional qualifications, although this was accompanied by the adoption of performance-based evaluation systems with an increased number of KPI elements. Many employees also emphasized the pressure of attempting to achieve ongoing improvement in productivity. For example, a number of formal contract employees of a DPE/IT service company (HNC6) in Changsha, Hunan Province, claimed there was "more overtime work in the past year" and "compared to previous years, the intensity of work is increasing, but still we get the same results for performance evaluation". Overall, responses on the impact of the reform on these employees' working life were negative and included views such as "working time is too long, leading to lower efficiency" and the reforms were "significantly affecting personal life and work motivation".

Not all workers were negative in their assessments of work and labour management. A number of formal contract employees in GDC5, a China-US joint venture company (JV/FIE) based in Guangzhou, were positive and claimed: "The service approaches have been changed, such as online customer service, WeChat and automatic voice systems. This has led to restructuring of positions within the company and our jobs have become more flexible and interesting". Other positive reforms mentioned included: "Changes to performance appraisal with an increase in bonus payment" and "As business changed, sales appraisal was added with customer service and our bonus was linked with customer satisfaction". In responding to the impact of these changes on their working life, most responses were positive, for instance, "Positive, more efficient and higher income". However, others saw these changes as having some positive as well as negative impacts, for example, "Positive with more income and negative with more pressure on performing well".

Given the mixed reaction to these changes, we asked workers to let us know what changes they would like to see. A number of employees of a SOE in Beijing (BJC3) responded with statements such as "Payment should be equal to employee's workload, the reason is a lot of staff have resigned because of this talent outflow", "The current leader should pay more attention on employees' benefits" and "Welfare, employee identity, enterprise value, and so on". Employees from a DPE in Beijing (BJC1) were also concerned about their real incomes falling due to inflation. As one worker suggested, "The company could offer reasonable wages to employees based on actual consumption index level and by monitoring our wage level in comparison with other similar companies' wage level". Clearly, many workers from SOEs and DPEs appear to be most concerned with adequate pay and employee benefits. In contrast, employees of BJC8, a JV/JSC, focused to a greater extent on wider management issues, such as "Improvements in cross department coordination", "Expect the company to explore new business opportunities that could lead to further development", "More training" and "Increases in employees' welfare". From these responses, we can see that employees of some companies were balancing their concerns between the company's future and their own individual well-being.

Workers in the south provided similar responses as well as alluding to some alternative suggestions on what needed to be done. Responses from employees of a DPE operating in Changsha (HNC6) included: "The company should pay for overtime work, since currently we don't have pay for overtime work, even on weekends", "Reducing working hours, particularly the overtime work" and "Improve management skill at bottom level, to increase work efficiency". The employees of the China-US JV/FIE in Guangzhou (GDC5) mentioned earlier suggested reform to management systems, such as improving the appraisal system and incentive effects, creating more career development channels for contract workers and enabling employees and the company to grow together, including focusing on remuneration and training. These different responses reflect the different concerns among employees with different locations and enterprise structures. Both DPE and SOE employees are more concerned with income and benefits, while employees in FIEs appear more concerned with improving the overall management system.

When asked about what they could do in order to help achieve the above changes, many workers responded by suggesting variations on the theme that they could work harder, be good at their job and develop feasible plans for the company's future development. These suggestions involve matters over which individual workers generally have some measure of control. Nevertheless, other workers extended their responses to encompass wider management activities, for instance, improving leadership capability and increasing developmental-oriented activities such as learning new skills and knowledge. Other employees were quite specific, recommending "providing suggestions to our managers and supervisors for improvement" as an effective way to achieve more positive change. In general, workers identified a number of key issues surrounding the impact of the reform process as well as some useful ways to mitigate some of the negative side effects. Such suggestions for future change did, however, vary significantly depending on firm location and enterprise structure.

Changes to pay, working time and other benefits

Changes to the organization of work have led to the reform of pay, working time and other benefits (see Min, Zhu and Bambacas, 2018) as well as to the five social insurances and the housing allowance as discussed in earlier chapters. These are sensitive issues for workers given that any reform of these conditions of employment will have a meaningful impact on employees' morale and motivation at the workplace (Warner and Zhu, 2018). In order to understand these issues from a worker's perspective, we asked participants in this project questions concerning the components of their wage, whether they received extra pay for overtime work, the number of hours they regularly worked, the amount of overtime work they now do compared to five years ago and whether they received any of the five social insurances or a housing allowance.

Workers' responses to questions concerning the overall wage components mirrored the responses of managers that were presented in Chapter 3. The major element was a basic wage component (the largest component) with consideration for skills, overtime pay, bonus, allowances and, for some managerial staff, an annualized salary. For example, employees of BJC3, a SOE, responded that their wage package was structured on the basis of "70 per cent basic wages and 30 per cent bonus and other benefits". For workers at BJC8, a JSC, the wage package was "60 per cent basic wages and 40 per cent bonus and other benefits". In contrast, employees of HBC5, a DPE, indicated that their wage was made up of "80 per cent basic wage and 20 per cent bonus and other benefits". FIEs appear to have less "pay at risk" as illustrated by the production workers of GDC6 whose pay was composed of "80 per cent basic wages, 10 per cent overtime pay, 5 per cent bonus and 5 per cent other benefits". The majority of enterprises appear to follow the legal requirement of paying employees for overtime work, although many of them calculated the rate based on the minimum wage level for the particular classification, not the average wage level as stipulated by the Labour Contract Law. At least one DPE, HNC6, appeared to breach this requirement and according to employees did not pay extra for overtime work.

Most firms had adopted the standard working hours, namely, 8 hours per day and 40 hours per week, as stipulated by legislation. The extent of working hours compliance did not, however, extend to overtime hours, which were unevenly allocated among different firms. From the survey results, we observed that the majority of SOEs, JSCs and FIEs reduced overtime work in accordance with the law, although many DPEs actually increased the overtime worked. This was evidenced, as demonstrated earlier in this chapter, by workers complaining about high levels of overtime worked and calling for either reduced overtime work or adequate overtime pay. In comparison with the working hours of five years ago, there was no change for regular hours, but for many companies, such as BJC3 and GDC6, overtime work had been reduced from more than 10 hours to less than 6 hours per week. Some DPEs, consistent with their unwillingness to pay for overtime hours as discussed above, increased or continued with overtime work exceeding 20 hours per week.

The payment of the five social insurances and housing allowance presents a more complex picture. The majority of companies (around 95 per cent) followed the relevant laws and regulations and paid the relevant social insurance expenses and housing allowance. As we discussed in Chapter 3, some firms did not, however, pay all five insurances for all workers. Employees of GDC7 (a Taiwanese investment firm – FIE) claimed that the company provided only partial compensation for non-resident workers on the basis that these employees did not have a local (Shenzhen) *hukou* and so were not entitled to unemployment and maternity insurance. In addition, some companies only covered their formal employees but not dispatched workers. Workers reported this was the case with GDC1, a DPE, which only paid the five insurances and housing allowance for contract workers (including non-local resident contract workers), but not dispatched workers, probably on the basis that this is the responsibility of the labour hire agent.

Changes to employment contract

Since the early years of reform, instituting a formal employment contract system has been one of the focal points in efforts by governments and the business community to eliminate labour abuse by employers of workers without the protection of regular employment (Zhu, Webber and Benson, 2010). In this research, we wanted to ascertain how widespread is the adoption of employment contracts, the form (written or oral contract) these contracts may take and the duration of the contracts. We were also interested in what has changed over the past five years and whether workers are happy with their own employment contract.

Nearly all the respondents to the survey had a written employment contract, although with some variation in the duration of the contract. In the north, employees of SOEs and JSCs (BJC3, BJC8 and HBC7) still had non-fixed term or permanent contracts for workers above 45 years of age, while younger employees normally had fixed-term contracts with a duration between three and five years. Over 98 per cent of DPE workers in the north were under fixed-term contracts with a duration between one and three years and with the possibility of renewal upon completion of the existing contract. Employees who were in management positions (HBC4 and HBC5) could be offered a non-fixed term contract. A similar situation was found in the south. For example, GDC7, a FIE, had three-year fixed term contracts for the majority of employees and non-fixed term contracts for managerial personnel. The adoption of three-year fixed-term contracts appeared to be the norm for the majority of employees of FIEs. This was not, however, the case for DPEs. In HNC6 and other DPEs in Hunan, 95 per cent of employees worked under a one-year contract with a renewal possible after each year. Overall, the evidence suggests that many SOEs still have non-fixed term contracts for their older employees due to time taken to phase out the old SOE employment contract system. Similarly, the overall duration of contracts appears to be longer in SOEs and FIEs (average between three and five years) in comparison with DPEs (average between one and three years). Managerial staff generally have obtained non-fixed term contracts regardless of ownership structure.

Contracts appear to have changed little compared to the situation five years ago. Over 95 per cent of workers reported there had been no major changes in the terms of the employment contract. Some minor changes occurred for individual workers due to the change from a permanent contract to the new terms of a non-fixed term contract. In excess of 98 per cent of workers indicated that they were happy with the current employment contract, although some workers expressed a contrary view. For example, a number of technicians in HBC9, a SOE, claimed that "the duration of the contract is too long, and we don't want to work here for too long." This comment suggests that workers with particular skills that are in demand would prefer more flexible contracts. For these workers, a long-term contract may lock them into their present employment and restrict their ability to pursue better opportunities with more pay. The situation is particularly relevant to many workers in SOEs, as their salary levels do not compete with many DPEs and FIEs for people with specialist skills. Leaving a job in a SOE before the end of a contract can, however, have some negative consequences, such as restrictions on transferring knowledge and technologies from that SOE to any new employer. Significant penalties could be imposed on those workers doing so.

Career development, training and promotion

In recent years, due to the increasing demand for skilled workers and the competition for talent (Min and Zhu, 2020), many companies have adopted HR practices focused on career development that have emphasized personal development, training and promotion (Min, Zhu and Bambacas, 2019). However, such opportunities may not be widespread and may vary considerably among different types of firms in China. In order to shed more light on how the macro-reform process may have led to changes at the enterprise level in these areas, we asked respondents questions concerning their chances of promotion and the factors that influence their promotion chances in their particular company (e.g. qualifications, experience, skill/knowledge, hardworking and loyalty), whether they had received training (e.g. job orientation, basic job training, position training, technical skills training and career path development planning) in the last 12 months, and what kind of training they now found most useful to them.

Workers' responses to these questions were associated with their job and position at their workplace. Generally, ordinary frontline workers received job orientation and basic job training. Employees with particular skills, such as technicians, normally received training beyond the basic sessions offered to ordinary workers, including position and technical skills training, in order to maintain and upgrade the skill level appropriate to their jobs. Sales staff normally received regular marketing training with up-to-date marketing information and selling skills programmes. Supervisors and managers usually received professional management training on various issues which would later give them the possibility to be promoted to higher positions.

Among our respondents, workers' perceptions about their chances of promotion related both to their companies' policy and to their own particular individual situation. In the north, employees of SOEs and JSCs, for example, BJC3 and BJC8, overwhelmingly felt that they had a chance of being promoted. This was in clear contrast to the majority of DPE workers, for example, BIC2 and HBC3, who felt they had little or no chance of promotion with their current employer. In the south, firms in Guangdong and Hunan, which were predominately FIEs and DPEs, also displayed such differences. Workers in FIEs, such as GDC5 and GDC7, felt they had access to promotion opportunities, although employees of other types of enterprises, such as GDC1 and HNC6, were pessimistic about their ability to gain a promotion. The overall situation indicates that SOEs, JSCs and FIEs generally provide more promotion opportunities to their employees than DPEs. One of the key reasons for this is that many DPEs are family-owned businesses and, as such, family members generally control the business, and other employees, who are often viewed as "outsiders", are seldom promoted.

If promotion is possible within the enterprise, workers are faced with important differences in the criteria used for promotion. Employees of SOEs, such as BJC3, ranked qualifications, skill/knowledge, loyalty/commitment and seniority as the key determining factors. Similarly, employees of JSCs, such as BJC8, ranked these factors as important with the addition of attitudes/personality and networks. Although employees of FIEs, such as GDC7, also agreed that qualifications, experience and skill/knowledge were important to their company, they also claimed that networks and being well trained were additional criteria. In short, all three enterprise forms placed considerable emphasis on qualifications and skills. In addition, SOEs also valued loyalty and seniority in promotion decisions, in contrast to FIEs which placed additional emphasis on experience, networks and being well trained. Clearly, SOEs, and to a certain degree JSCs, still follow some path-dependent practices related to the old Chinese personnel management approach, whilst unsurprisingly FIEs are more orientated towards modern HR practices with a focus on individual competency and capabilities.

Training and development appeared to be important to the vast majority of enterprises with 98 per cent of workers indicating job orientation and basic job training were adopted by their companies. In BJC1, a DPE, most employees also obtained position training as well as specialized skills training for technicians and management training and career path development planning for engineers and employees with a supervisory role. For employees working in SOEs and JSCs, such as BJC3 and BJC8, training focused on position, political and technical skills instruction, whilst supervisors were offered management training. Similar training arrangements also occurred among FIEs, with the important addition of occupational health and safety training (OH&S). Many FIEs, for example, GDC3, GDC5, GDC7 and GDC9, placed considerable importance on OH&S training for all employees, which sets them apart from SOEs, JSCs and DPEs, where such training was not mentioned by employees.

The value of the training offered was assessed differently by workers depending on their rank and position in the enterprise. For the regular worker, job orientation, on-the-job training, job rotation and basic skills training were considered very useful, whereas for technicians more specialized technical skills training and career path development were considered important. Employees with a supervisory role or occupying a management position generally valued specialist management programmes and career planning.

Relationships with management

The relationship between workers and management has grown in importance in recent years due to the difficulties in attracting and retaining the younger generation of employees (Ren, Xie, Zhu and Warner, 2018). In response, many companies have adopted strategic HRM practices and, in particular, high performance work systems (HPWS). This move, it is believed, will allow employees to participate in management decision-making and encourage managers to have a more open and caring management style towards employees (Min, Zhu and Bambacas, 2018). In this research, we explored how this situation has changed in recent years. In particular, we asked workers about the avenues available to them to express their concerns or thoughts to management (such avenues could include the direct supervisor, team members, the HR department, senior management, trade unions, workplace meetings, suggestion schemes and employee surveys), and what they thought were the most effective ways to communicate with management.

Employees at SOEs and JSCs, for example, BJC3 and BJC8, indicated there were multiple channels they considered useful to express their concerns to management, including direct supervisor, HR department, suggestion schemes and employee survey. In contrast, employees at DPEs, for example, HBC3, HBC4 and HNC6, suggested direct supervisor and HR department as preferred avenues for them to express their point of view. Other employees working for JV/FIEs, such as GDC5 and GDC7, suggested that they had many avenues for expressing their concerns, such as direct supervisor, team members, HR department, workplace meetings and employee surveys. Overall, however, it appeared that the vast majority of employees perceived the most effective way to communicate with management was either through their direct supervisor or through the HR department.

Conclusion

In order to analyze the impact of macro-economic policy at the enterprise level, this chapter focused on the employees' experiences of, and responses to, labour management reform and management practices within their firm. Based on survey data collected from employees working in 60 enterprises with different ownership structures, namely, SOEs, JSCs, DPEs and FIEs, and located in the north (Beijing and Hebei) and the south (Guangdong and Hunan), we explored the different responses of employees in five key areas: macro-economic reform and the impact on employees due to corresponding changes in company-level labour management; changes to pay, working time and other benefits; changes to employment contracts; career development; and relationships with management. These themes and some representative employees' responses are presented in Table 4.1.

Given the increasing effort made by governments at all levels (both central and local governments) to effectively implement and enforce new labour laws and regulations, most employees in the different types of enterprises considered in this research had experienced many positive changes, such as increasing wages and overall income level, enhanced social insurance coverage and improvement in other benefits. For many workers, training and career development had also been adopted in their firms and employees could utilize such opportunities according to their position and professional status. Workers have also become more aware of their statutory rights and obligations, and hence they are more likely to act accordingly, such as expressing their concerns with direct supervisors, HR department and other communication pathways. The analysis of employees' responses undertaken in this chapter has generated a number of findings that are generally consistent with the views of management as detailed in Chapter 3. This was particularly the case relating to the increasing utilization of institutional mechanisms and the "rule of law" oriented labour management practices.

Owing to the widespread shortages of labour, however, there is a trend towards a more diverse workforce consisting of a combination of dispatched

Table 4.1 Employees' responses to labour management reform and management practices in China

Themes	Key employees' responses
Economic reform and key changes of labour management	1 *What has been the one key change in terms of organization of work in the last five years (i.e. positive vs. negative)?* Employees of SOEs and JSC claimed more positive changes: "adjustment of working hours, reduced working time"; "get promoted"; "less on overtime work and more on wages increase". Employees of DPEs claimed more negative changes: "more overtime work, and more pressure on performing well with possible deduction of bonus and other benefits if we don't perform well". Employees of JVs/FIEs claimed mixed changes: "jobs become more flexible and interesting"; "changes of performance appraisal with increase of bonus payment"; "more end year incentive bonus but with heavier workload". SOEs, JSCs and JVs/FIEs provided better working conditions, less overtime work and relatively secure social insurances and other benefits in comparison with many DPEs. Companies located in the southern region (i.e. Guangdong) tended to have more overtime work, flexible work arrangements and more pressure on work performance linked to the incentive pay than the companies located in the northern and inland regions. 2 *What change would you like to see and how do you achieve this change?* Employees in SOEs were more concerned with adequate pay and employee benefits. Employees in JSCs had mixed concerns regarding both organizational and individual well-being. Employees in DPEs were more concerned with their wages and overall income level. Employees in JVs/FIEs were more concerned with improving management systems and individual career development. 3 *What can you do in order to make changes?* "Working hard" and "be good at my own job, think about feasible plans for the company's future development" were common answers. *(Continued)*

Table 4.1 (Continued)

Themes	Key employees' responses
	Others emphasized "improving leadership capability" and "keep learning new skills and knowledge" as a more developmental-oriented approach.
	Some employees also mentioned "providing suggestions to our managers and supervisors for improvement" as the effective way for future changes.
Changes to pay, working time and other benefits	1 *What are the components of your wage?*
	The majority of components included: larger proportion of basic wages, different arrangements of skill and post wage, overtime pay, bonus, allowances, and for some people with management positions, annual salary could be an option.
	2 *Do you receive extra pay for overtime work?*
	Employees of majority of firms, namely, SOEs, JSCs and FIEs/JVs, received pay for overtime work, but a number of DPEs did not pay overtime work.
	3 *How many regular hours and overtime work do you work a day in comparison to five years ago?*
	Most firms have adopted 8 hours per day and 40 hours per week as regular hours stipulated by the government. However, overtime hours were not evenly distributed among different firms.
	The majority of SOEs, JSCs and FIEs adopted less overtime work by following the new regulation, but many DPEs increased the amount of overtime work.
	In comparison to five years ago, many firms reduced their overall working hours through the reduction of overtime work, but many DPEs increased their overtime work.
	4 *Do you receive any social insurances and housing allowances?*
	The majority of firms paid the five insurances and housing allowances, but some firms did not pay certain elements of the insurances or housing allowances for non-local resident employees or dispatched workers.

Themes	Key employees' responses
Changes to employment contracts	1 *How widespread has the adoption of employment contracts been, in which form and for how long?* Almost all employees had a written employment contract, but with different durations. SOEs and JSCs still had non-fixed term contracts or permanent contracts for the older employees (e.g. age above 45), while for the younger employees, they normally had fixed-term contracts with a duration between three and five years. Employees of DPEs were under fixed-term contracts with a duration between one and three years with possible renewal of the contract thereafter. Employees of JVs/FIEs were under fixed-term contracts with a duration of three years and renewable thereafter. 2 *What has changed in comparison with five years ago and are you happy with the employment contract?* Not many changes were noted. Most people were happy with their employment contract, although some SOE employees (i.e. technicians) complained that the contract duration was too long and not easy for them to quit and change to another job.
Career development	1 *Do you have any chance of being promoted in this company?* Employees' responses were associated with their job and position at their workplace. Employees of SOEs and JSCs overwhelmingly responded "Yes". A "No" answer was more typical of the majority of employees of DPEs. Some employees in JVs/FIEs responded "Yes" regarding promotion opportunity, but many employees responded "No". 2 *What factors will influence your chances of getting promoted in this company?* Employees of SOEs indicated "qualifications, skill/knowledge, loyalty/commitment and seniority". Employees of JSCs indicated "experience, attitude, skill/knowledge, networks, loyalty/commitment and seniority".

(Continued)

Table 4.1 (Continued)

Themes	Key employees' responses
	Employees of JVs/FIEs indicated "qualifications, experience, skill/knowledge, networks and being well trained".
	3 *Have you received training on the following activities in the last 12 months?* The majority of responses indicated "job orientation training and basic job training". "Position training" and "technical skills training" for technicians. "Management training" and "career path development planning" for people with supervisor roles and engineers. "Marketing training" for salespeople. JVs/FIEs also focused on OH&S training, but this was not the case for other firms.
	4 *What kind of training is most useful for you now?* For ordinary workers, job orientation, on the job training, job rotation and basic skills training were seen as useful. For technicians, technical skills training and career path development training were important. For people with supervisor roles or in management positions, management training and career planning were important and useful.
Relationships with management	1 *Do you use any of these avenues to express your concerns or thoughts to management?* Employees of SOEs and JSCs indicated "direct supervisor, HR department, suggestion schemes and employees survey". Employees of DPEs indicated "direct supervisor and HR department". Employees of JVs/FIEs indicated "direct supervisor, team members, HR department, workplace meetings and employee surveys".
	2 *Which way is the most effective one to communicate with management?* Most employees expressed the two most effective ways were directly through their supervisor or HR department.

Source: Worker survey.

workers, non-local resident contract workers and regular local formal contract workers. One general outcome is labour segmentation with different treatment between dispatched workers and other contract workers (including non-local resident and local resident contract workers), where the former group is managed by labour hire companies and work conditions are arranged under fixed contracts and entitlements with the relevant agents. This explains why many dispatched workers reported "no changes" to many of the questions related to the impact of enterprise-level reform. However, regular contract workers, irrespective of whether they were local or non-local residents, experienced many significant changes at their workplace. As a consequence, in this chapter, we mainly focused on those workers, comparing and contrasting their different experiences and responses by breaking down the analysis by enterprise location and ownership.

Table 4.1 shows the major responses with the different regions and enterprise ownership highlighted. Generally, our research demonstrates some important ownership differences as well as locational differences (south vs. north) concerning the overall impact of new management practices on employees. The key impacts of the micro-level enterprise reform include: first, SOEs, JSCs and FIEs provided better working conditions, less overtime work and relatively secure social insurances and other benefits in comparison with most DPEs. Second, enterprises located in the south (Guangdong) tended to have more overtime work, flexible work arrangements and more pressure placed on employees' work performance based on the stronger link to performance pay than firms located in the northern and inland regions.

The overall pay system appears to be differentiated by enterprise ownership where SOEs have adopted a more traditionally oriented pay package in comparison with privately owned firms, particularly FIEs which place more weight on employee performance. Other working conditions, such as normal working hours, as discussed in Chapter 3, have been standardized across China since the implementation of the new Labour Contract Law, which specifies a standard 8 hours per day and 40 hours per week. Notwithstanding, overtime work and pay varies significantly between different types of firms. The majority of companies provided the five social insurances and one housing allowance for most of their employees, but disparities existed and discrimination towards dispatched and non-local resident workers continues. Moreover, whilst training and career development has become more widespread and available, employees in SOEs, JSCs and FIEs seemed to have better access to such developmental opportunities than workers in their DPE counterparts.

Similarly, companies located in the more southern, opened economic regions (e.g. Guangdong) appeared to have introduced more avenues for employee participation in management decisions. This has enabled workers from the south to express their concerns directly to supervisors and managers when compared to companies located in the north and inland regions. Such practices were also more prevalent in FIEs due to the likelihood of importation of international HR best practices. In addition, SOEs and JSCs appeared to maintain a number of traditional HR practices in which seniority, loyalty and networks are important factors for people to be promoted in contrast to FIEs where capability and competency are more important factors for advancement.

In summary, the overall trajectory of labour management reform is towards more institutionalized, modernized and internationalized systems and practices. This outcome has, however, been met with mixed responses from employees – positive responses related to increases in pay, improved social insurance coverage, flexible work arrangements and training and career development, but negative worker responses to higher workloads and the increased pressure to perform well through higher levels of productivity and efficiency. Employees also expressed concerns about the prospects of maintaining traditional employment equities and justice alongside the ongoing reform agenda. This concern and whether workers feel they are being fairly treated under the impact of the macro-economic reform agenda will be addressed in Chapter 5.

5 Regular workers and perceptions of fairness

Introduction

As discussed in earlier chapters, the reform of the past four decades has had significant impact on society and enterprises, as well as on individual employees and their working life. One consequence has been the increasing social disparity reflected through inequality of employees' income and working conditions (Zhu, Warner and Feng, 2011). As documented in Chapter 1, the Gini coefficient for China of 0.475 (NBS, 2017) is well above the warning level of 0.40 for maintaining political, social and economic stability. Such disparity has led commentators to question whether the market-focused economic reform in China is sustainable at both the societal level and the workplace level.

Any disparity and inequality among workers will impact on their perceptions of, and responses to, what they might consider fair and just at the workplace, particularly during periods of economic and societal transformation. Under different economic systems, fairness or justice (we will use the two concepts interchangeably in this chapter; see Konovsky, 2000) may have different underpinnings and individual employees may also have different preferences. In China, for example, the income distribution system under the planned economy was principally underpinned by equality-based distributive justice that emphasized the principle of equal pay for employees with similar jobs and positions in the workplace. This system did not on the whole consider the contributions made by different employees. Manual workers were divided into a number of ranking categories and generally received the same wages at the same ranking level (Zhu and Warner, 2004), although some minor variations in pay did occur.

The income distribution system, with its focus on 'equal pay', became a key part of the reform agenda and resulted in a shift from an equality-oriented to an equity-oriented approach with the emphasis placed on measuring individual workers' contributions and paying them accordingly. This shift was achieved through pay systems such as piece rates, hourly rates and a combination of a basic wage plus position and incentive pay (i.e. the so-called structural or floating wage system) (Zhu and Warner, 2004).

With these changes, management aimed to reward employees based on their contribution to the enterprise rather than simply paying them for doing similar work. By doing so, at least in theory, enterprises could achieve higher productivity and production outcomes, and the overall economic system could become more efficient (Zhu and Warner, 2004). However, the standards being set for measuring and rewarding individual employees' work coupled with other reformed management systems and practices, such as the role of the supervisor, have led to higher targets, more restrictive work conditions and increased demands from management.

The aim of this chapter is to explore how the macro reforms have impacted on employees' perceptions of and responses to what they consider as workplace fairness. We will focus on employees' evaluation of the relevant changes in the organization of work, including salaries, work conditions, work intensity and job security. Workers' perceptions regarding the fairness of relevant changes, new standards/measurement, the treatment from their supervisors and their overall satisfaction with the current working conditions and jobs will also be examined.

Before undertaking the analysis, it is important to be clear about what is meant by fairness and justice at workplace and understand the underpinning literature related to the various forms of justice: distributive, procedural and interactional. Distributive justice provides the fundamental basis of employees' evaluation of the gains from employment and whether such distribution rules are understood (Cohen, 1987). Procedural justice, on the other hand, refers to the perceived fairness of the decision process leading to the distributive outcomes with both objective and subjective circumstances (Konovsky, 2000). Interactional justice connotes the personal tenor of supervisor-subordinate relations, reflecting whether employees perceive that supervisors support and respect them (Collins and Mossholder, 2014).

The next section will thus present a brief review of the relevant justice literature by focusing on the issue of employees' perceptions and responses regarding the fairness of the key changes in the organization of work, the fairness of pay and working conditions and the fairness of supervisors' actions at workplace. In addition, individual workers' perception regarding workplace fairness arising from comparisons with others also provides some understanding of the fairness issue from an employee's perspective. We will present the key research questions based on the relevant literature. After a brief note on the data, the chapter will examine the survey results with an analysis of employees who have different locations, employment contracts, demographics and employment. The chapter concludes by relating the findings to the continuing economic reform taking place in China.

Fairness and justice at the workplace

The challenge for decision-makers within governments and enterprises is employees' concern with what they may perceive as unfair treatment at the workplace that has emanated from the reform agenda. The negative perceptions that such treatment might engender and the subsequent responses of employees could lead to less productive outcomes and, in the long run, challenge the sustainability of the business operation, negatively impacting on the efficacy of the ongoing market economic reform (Zhu and Webber, 2017).

The early literature on organizational fairness/justice emphasized the role of distributive justice or the fairness of the distribution of organizational outcomes (Bierhoff, Cohen and Greenberg, 1986; Collins and Mossholder, 2014). Economic reform in China led to a change in the underpinning principles of the distributive reward system from equality to equity. These two principles are rooted in different theoretical perspectives. Equality theory suggests individual employees should be rewarded equally regardless of their inputs (Deutsch, 1985). This would be considered fair as individual employees would receive the same reward for doing the same job at the same ranking level. In contrast, equity theory suggests that individual employees evaluate the distribution of outcomes by comparing one's input and achieved outcomes relative to a referent comparison (Greenberg, Ashton-James and Ashkanasy, 2007). Thus, the fairness of outcomes would be determined by individual employees comparing their rewards with a salient referent standard, which they derive based on prior experiences, expectations or by reference to other workers (Greenberg, Ashton-James and Ashkanasy, 2007). The process of evaluation of equitable rewards can produce emotions which, it is argued, motivate employees to change their behaviour or cognitions associated with a positive response, such as being happy with the work and working conditions as well as higher levels of job satisfaction. In contrast, an inequitable evaluation is more likely to lead to a negative emotional reaction, such as job dissatisfaction, distress, reduced well-being and respect for their jobs, and increased intentions to quit (Collins and Mossholder, 2014; Stone-Romero and Stone, 2005; Tepper, 2001; van Dierendonck, Schaufeli and Buunk, 2001).

Distributive justice theories thus provide a strong underpinning for this chapter as they allow for the examination of employees' overall perceptions and responses with regard to the changes in the distributive system and standards (from equality to equity-based principles) arising from economic reform. The key issue thus becomes whether this reform has led to workers viewing the outcomes as fair and whether they feel better off compared to others.

In distributing rewards to various stakeholders, management must ensure that employees have some understanding of the underpinning processes involved. Procedural justice theories thus are concerned with the perceived fairness of processes used in making decisions about rewards and benefits (Folger and Greenberg, 1985). This provides a different perspective with which to investigate individual employees' perceptions towards policy changes and management decisions that influence employees' working life

(Lee and Jensen, 2014; Walumbwa, Hartnell and Misati, 2017). Generally, procedural justice refers to how an allocation decision is made and can be viewed objectively or subjectively (Konovsky, 2000). Objective procedural justice refers to actual or factual processes (Lind, 2001; Lind and Tyler, 1988), whilst subjective procedural justice refers to perceptions of a process or the process's capacity to enhance fairness judgements (Konovsky and Cropanzano, 1991).

Subjective or procedural justice perceptions can be understood by considering the cognitive, affective and behavioural components of the justice episode (Leventhal, Karuza and Fry, 1980). The cognitive component refers to the calculations made by an employee regarding the objective fairness of a policy or decision; the affective component consists of positive or negative emotional reaction to actual events; and the behavioural component leads to important positive or negative consequences of employee behaviour and attitudes, such as job satisfaction (Bies and Tripp, 1996; Lee and Jensen, 2014; Skarlicki and Folger, 1997). In this study, individual employees' perceptions regarding the impact of changes to the organization of work can be seen as subjective procedural justice (Lee and Jensen, 2014). If employees are satisfied with the new management systems and practices, they will respond with positive emotional responses and reactions.

More recent research on fairness has focused on interactional justice that explores whether supervisors treat employees fairly (Collins and Mossholder, 2014). Interactions between supervisors and subordinates can be complex to understand, but the key issue is whether employees feel their supervisors treat them with respect and support, thus validating the organizational standing of these employees (Bies, 2001). If supervisors promote positive relational norms and are seen to be fair, employees will be encouraged to reciprocate with positive work behaviours (Korsgaard, Meglino, Lester and Jeong, 2010). In this study, individual employees' perceptions regarding their supervisors' treatment and whether their supervisors are supportive and caring will be the prime measure of employee perceived interactional justice.

Using the above broad perspectives concerning fairness and justice, this chapter will address the following two key questions. First, how fair do employees see the outcomes of the reform process in terms of procedural, distributive and interactional fairness or justice? These three perspectives provide a useful way to ascertain the fairness perceptions of workers. Second, are employees satisfied with their job and current working conditions? This last question is important as it provides an overall employee assessment of the impact of the reforms on their working life.

Data

The two research questions presented above give rise to four themes that will underpin this chapter on employees' perceptions of fairness. These themes and the corresponding survey questions are detailed in Table 5.1. The wider research methodology utilized to gather this data was discussed in Chapter 1. The survey included questions regarding employees' perceived (subjective) procedural fairness on changes to the organization of work, distributive fairness of pay and working conditions, interactional fairness of supervisors' support and treatment, as well as employees' overall satisfaction with working conditions and jobs.

The employees surveyed for this research were diverse in terms of location (northern China, southern China), employment type (contract arrangement), personal characteristics (age, gender, educational qualifications and professional/occupational certification), household registration (urban or rural, local or migrant) and enterprise structure. Location is included in this analysis as, in certain cases, the proximity to the political centre (i.e. Beijing) may have influenced workers' acceptance of the key policy changes relating to the organization of work. Details of these variables were presented in Chapter 1 (see Table 1.2). It is likely that such differences will lead to variations in the experience and satisfaction with economic reform. As a key aim of the book is to identify similar and different perceptions and responses among employees, the discussion in this chapter will break down the analysis based on these differences.

Perceptions of fairness and employee satisfaction

As outlined in Tables 5.1, we used a number of questions to assess the various forms of fairness (procedural, distributive and interaction) and employees' overall satisfaction with their job and working conditions. The results of the research are documented in Tables 5.2 and 5.3. Table 5.2 explores the key themes broken down by the north (Beijing and Hebei) and south (Hunan and Guangdong) regions. Table 5.3 extends this analysis by breaking down perceived fairness and satisfaction with job and employment conditions by location, various employee demographics and enterprise structure.

Procedural fairness

Procedural fairness or justice is often the starting point for employees in assessing fairness in the workplace as it ultimately underpins decisions about the distribution of rewards. Such fairness is difficult to assess, particularly when most of the organizational-level changes emanated from central government in the form of statutes and regulations. Implementation of such policies was, in some cases, modified by provincial and city level governments, which could explain some of the variance in responses between the regions surveyed.

Sixty per cent of employees in the south (Hunan and Guangdong) were more likely to view the policy changes as having a positive influence on the enterprise compared to 49 per cent of employees in the north (Beijing and Hebei). Only 9 per cent of employees in both regions saw such reform in a

Table 5.1 Research themes and worker survey questions

Research themes	Survey questions
Employees' perceived (subjective) procedural fairness on changes to the organization of work	• What has been the one key change in terms of organization of work in the last five years? • How has this change affected your working life • Overall, has this been good or bad for you? • If bad, what did you do about it? • Did this change affect you more or less than most other people who work in this company?
Employees' perceived distributive fairness regarding pay and employment conditions	• Are you paid more, about the same or less than other people doing a similar job? • Compared to others in this company with a similar job and qualification – for regular working hours per day, do you: a. work more; b. same; c. less • Compared to others in this company with a similar job and qualification – for regular working days per week, do you: a. work more; b. same; c. less • Compared to others in this company with a similar job and qualification – for overtime work per week, do you: a. work more; b. same; c. less • Compared to others in this company with a similar job and qualification – for other benefits and allowances, do you: a. get more; b. same; c. less; d. unsure • Compared to others in this company with a similar job and qualification – for your own contribution to social insurance, do you: a. pay more; b. same; c. less; d. unsure • Compared to others in this company with a similar job and qualification – for the company's contribution to social insurance for you, do they: a. pay more; b. same; c. less; d. unsure • Compared to others in this company with a similar job and qualification – for the employment contract, do you: a. have longer contracts; b. same; c. shorter; d. unsure • Compared to others in this company with a similar job and qualification – for promotion opportunities, do you: a. have more chances; b. same; c. less; d. unsure

Research themes	Survey questions
Employees' perceived interactional fairness regarding supervisors' support and treatment	• Compared to others in this company with a similar job and qualification – for training opportunities, do you: a. have more chances; b. same; c. less; d. unsure • I can fully participate in decisions made by my supervisor. • My supervisor is willing to listen to work-related problems. • I feel free to discuss job-related problems with my supervisor. • I am comfortable expressing my feelings to my supervisor. • My supervisor can be relied on when things get difficult at work. • My supervisor is very concerned about the welfare of those under him/her.
Employee satisfaction with job and working conditions	• Are you happy with the terms and conditions of your employment? • I find real satisfaction in my job.

Source: Worker survey.

negative light. Interestingly, employees in the north were more likely to assess the reforms as having no influence on the enterprise (42 per cent) compared to employees in the south (31 per cent). Part of the explanation for this subjective assessment of procedural fairness may be that the take-up of the reform agenda was slower further away from the political centre of gravity and thus workers in the south had more time to transition to any new arrangements.

The above findings could also relate to whether the resultant organizational changes had some influence on the employees' working life. This more objective form of assessment allowed employees to relate the changes to their own particular circumstances. Most employees perceived only an average impact on their working life, although this was slightly more pronounced in the south (61 per cent) than in the north (54 per cent). Importantly, for those who responded that reform had a high level of influence on their working life, the respective figures were 23 per cent (south) and 21 per cent (north). This suggests that the reform agenda had fewer negative consequences for workers in the north than for their counterparts in the south and hence was perhaps more in line with enterprise practices in that region. These workers possibly also felt they had been informed or consulted of such changes, resulting in a perception of procedural fairness. Overall, we can conclude that the impact of overall policy changes on the organization of work have had a positive impact on employees, although some differences do exist between northern and southern regions.

Table 5.2 Employees' perceived fairness and satisfaction with jobs and working conditions by region (%)

Key themes	North (Beijing and Hebei)			South (Hunan and Guangdong)		
Employees' perceptions of the influence of the key policy changes	*Positive influence*	*Negative influence*	*No influence*	*Positive influence*	*Negative influence*	*No influence*
On the organization of work	49	9	42	60	9	31
	High	*Average*	*Low*	*High*	*Average*	*Low*
On their working life	21	54	25	23	61	16
Employees' perceived fairness of working conditions	*Fair*	*Unfair*	*Unsure*	*Fair*	*Unfair*	*Unsure*
Overall payment (including all benefits)	35	49	16	53	36	10
Working hours per day	80	19	1	76	16	9
Overtime per week	62	21	17	71	13	16
Wages	58	6	36	76	6	18
Other benefits	59	10	31	95	5	9
Self-contributed insurance	58	2	40	74	2	23
Company paid insurance	48	6	46	63	5	32
Job contract	71	5	24	86	1	13
Promotion	56	12	32	71	12	17
Training	65	12	23	85	6	9
Supervisor support	*Satisfied*	*Unsure*	*Not satisfied*	*Satisfied*	*Unsure*	*Not satisfied*
Employees' overall satisfaction regarding supervisors' support and treatment	83	–	17	76	–	24
Employee satisfaction	*Satisfied*	*Unsure*	*Not satisfied*	*Satisfied*	*Unsure*	*Not satisfied*
Employees' overall satisfaction with job and conditions of work	42	41	17	87	11	2

Source: Worker survey.

In order to explore these policy impacts further, employees were asked the question: "What have been the major policy changes in the last five years?" A number of key areas were articulated by employees included in responses, such as: the organizational structure has been streamlined with more efficient structures and systems, employees need to perform well and compete for their positions, more performance-based assessment with more detailed

Table 5.3 Employees' overall perceived fairness and satisfaction with jobs and working conditions (%)

	Overall income			Working hours per day			Wages			Other benefits		
	Fair	Unfair	Unsure	Fair	Unfair	Unsure	Fair	Unfair	Unsure	Fair	Unfair	Unsure
Worker type												
Dispatched workers	20	20	60	0	0	100	100	0	0	75	0	25
Contract workers	35	50	15	1	20	79	57	7	36	58	11	31
Age												
<35 years old	37	46	17	2	18	80	52	7	41	56	9	35
35–45	34	49	18	0	41	59	69	6	24	67	15	18
>45 years old	29	71	0	0	19	81	74	4	22	66	13	22
Gender												
Male	36	50	15	37	15	49	60	7	33	65	11	24
Female	35	48	17	1	16	82	56	6	38	53	10	37
Education												
Tertiary and above	28	57	15	2	0	98	56	7	37	56	13	31
Below tertiary	44	40	16	1	22	77	59	6	35	61	8	31
Local Hukou status												
Yes	31	54	15	2	0	98	65	5	30	60	12	28
No	43	39	18	2	28	70	44	8	48	55	8	37
Urban/rural citizen												
Urban	32	55	12	2	17	81	62	7	31	63	11	26
Rural	42	33	24	0	25	75	47	5	48	47	8	44
Certification												
Yes	33	52	15	0	19	81	61	5	34	58	10	32
No	36	47	16	2	20	78	54	7	38	59	10	31
Enterprise ownership												
SOEs	19	61	20	0	18	82	58	7	35	62	12	27
DPEs	43	44	13	1	20	79	55	8	37	56	11	34

(Continued)

Table 5.3 (Continued)

	Overall income			Working hours per day			Wages			Other benefits			Overall satisfaction	
	Fair	*Unfair*	*Unsure*	*Fair*	*Unfair*	*Unsure*	*Fair*	*Unfair*	*Unsure*	*Fair*	*Unfair*	*Unsure*	*High*	*Low*
FIEs	37	43	20	34	12	54	51	4	45	55	9	36	60	40
JSCs	55	45	0	0	55	45	91	9	0	100	0	0	83	17

	Contract arrangement			Promotion opportunities			Training arrangement			Interactional fairness			Overall satisfaction	
	Fair	*Unfair*	*Unsure*	*Fair*	*Unfair*	*Unsure*	*Fair*	*Unfair*	*Unsure*	*Fair*	*Unfair*	*Unsure*	*High*	*Low*
Worker type														
Dispatched workers	100	0	0	100	0	0	100	0	0	70	30	0		
Contract workers	71	5	24	65	13	22	56	12	32	73	20	7		
Age														
<35 years old	72	4	24	62	11	27	58	10	32	65	15	20	81	19
35–45	69	4	27	69	8	23	69	4	27	85	8	7	85	15
>45 years old	71	10	19	65	35	0	71	10	19	65	25	10	85	15
Gender														
Male	74	4	22	67	13	20	59	11	30	73	13	14	61	39
Female	78	6	16	64	11	25	68	5	27	68	11	21	60	40
Education														
Tertiary and above	66	5	29	62	14	24	66	4	29	75	14	11	77	23
Below tertiary	67	4	29	69	10	21	67	4	29	82	10	8	89	11
Local Hukou status														
Yes	75	6	20	68	12	20	54	13	33	83	12	5	84	16
No	65	2	33	60	12	28	65	2	33	69	12	19	81	19
Urban/rural citizen														
Urban	71	6	23	65	14	21	56	13	32	65	14	21	83	17
Rural	71	0	29	66	8	26	71	0	29	66	8	26	83	17
Certification														
Yes	65	8	27	70	12	18	57	11	32	80	12	8	80	20

No	75	3	22	61	12	27	64	3	23	69	12	19	84	16
Enterprise ownership														
SOEs	70	7	23	61	19	20	40	20	40	83	10	10	52	48
DPEs	71	2	27	67	10	23	71	2	27	70	10	20	61	39
FIEs	74	0	27	64	9	27	73	0	27	80	9	11	60	40
JSCs	81	0	9	91	9	0	91	0	9	84	9	7	81	19

Source: Worker survey.

KPI items is needed, increased wage and other benefits (e.g. holiday bonus and paid vacation) were associated with increased workloads and improved performance and overall productivity, job contents have changed substantially with more detailed description of duties and responsibilities, and more job-related training and career planning are required (based on different interviewees' responses). These responses generally indicate the adoption of the so-called 'modern management system' with an emphasis on efficiency, productivity and performance-based rewards which had, in the main, generated higher wages among the majority of workers. The findings provide support to the view expressed above that the policy changes generated support among employees.

In order to explore these responses further, we asked employees the question: "What are the most important policy changes you want to see?" This question was intended to assist in assessing the procedural fairness of the reforms by ascertaining whether reforms important to workers had been neglected. The majority of employees wanted to see more efficient management systems, more productive outcomes, the expansion of business scope and better wages and benefits. Clearly, there is close alignment between the reform agenda and employees' expectations, namely, a focus on the better economic performance of firms that, in turn, leads to better pay and benefits for workers. When asked: "How do you achieve these changes?", employees' responses included: through hard work, commitment to work, better leadership, learning more new things to improve innovative capability and exploring new markets and business opportunities. These comments suggest that most workers would be willing to initiate change where possible as can be seen in workers' responses to the question: "Which organizations or channels would you engage to raise your concerns about reform issues?" Responses included: local union branches, local district committees, local labour bureaus, and media outlets and social media. The majority of responses were not, however, directly related to their workplace management, particularly their senior management team. However, when workers were asked, "Which channels are most useful for you to express concerns regarding the management issues at your workplace?", responses included: direct supervisors, company union branches, employees' suggestion schemes, followed by the HR department and senior management team. With an overall positive response towards supervisors' support and treatment (83 per cent and 76 per cent in the north and south, respectively), the strong relationships between managers/supervisors and workers suggest employees have a strong sense of procedural fairness.

Finally, when workers were asked, "Which government agencies were most effective in protecting your interests?", the majority of employees responded in the following order: local labour bureau and arbitration agents, local people's court and local people's complaint bureau. These responses suggest that workers were becoming familiar with the relevant legal processes as the primary means for protecting their rights and interests through mechanisms such as arbitration and the court system.

Distributive fairness

In order to understand employees' perceptions of the fairness of rewards distribution in their enterprise, we examined a number of key indicators, namely, overall payment (including benefits), working hours per day, overtime per week, wages, other benefits, self-contributed insurance and company paid insurance (including the five types of social insurance: pension, medical, unemployment, maternity and work-related injury insurance), the job contract, promotion opportunities and training arrangements. When broken down by location, employee demographics and enterprise structure, some significant differences were revealed.

Location mattered in several of the key indicators. For example, 49 per cent of employees in the north claimed the overall payment was unfair compared with only 36 per cent employees in the south. Similarly, fewer people in the north perceived overtime hours per week as being fair: 62 per cent in the north and 71 per cent in the south. On the other hand, more employees in the south felt wages and other benefits were fair (76 per cent and 95 per cent, respectively) in comparison with their counterparts in the north (58 per cent and 59 per cent, respectively). This trend continued with a range of other issues, such as self-contributed insurance, company paid insurance, job contract, promotion opportunities and training arrangements. In these cases, from 10 to 20 per cent more employees from the south felt the benefits were fair compared to employees from the north. With regard to other issues, few differences distinguished workers from either region. For example, employees' perceptions of fairness of working hours were similar in the north and south (80 per cent and 76 per cent, respectively).

There are a number of explanations for such regional differences. First, per capita income is significantly higher in Beijing (see Table 1.1) and this would, at least to some degree, influence workers' perceptions of what constitutes fair rewards in the north. In other words, their reference point may be less related to their own industry and more to the highly paid sectors. Second, employees in the south work for companies that are more open to global markets with a longer history of adopting an 'open door' policy and experiencing overall industrial prosperity, relatively higher income levels and more international-oriented HR practices. These factors could influence employees in the south to adopt more positive responses towards questions concerning the overall fairness of wages and working conditions than those in the north. Third, the demographic composition of respondent employees is quite different in several important respects between the two regions. This difference is illustrated in Table 1.2 which shows that respondent employees in the south were more likely to be male and professionally qualified, whist respondents in the north were more likely to be contract workers with a local *hukou* and an urban citizenship.

In order to explore these demographic differences further, we analyzed the findings by breaking employees into different categories, such as dispatched workers and formal contract workers, employees in different age groups (i.e. below 35, between 35 and 45, and above 45), gender, education (i.e. tertiary and below tertiary), permanent residence with local *hukou* or migrant workers without local *hukou*, employees with urban or rural citizenship status, employees with or without professional certification and the ownership structure of the enterprise. As can be seen in Table 5.3, employees with different personal background reacted differently to questions regarding the overall perceived fairness of wages and working conditions.

We begin this discussion on the potential impact of employee characteristics on distributive fairness or justice by comparing dispatched workers with contract workers. Contract workers generally have more security and prestige in the organization, although dispatched workers may be grateful to the host company for providing work, thereby retaining their jobs. Contract workers were more likely to perceive overall income as fair compared to dispatched workers (35 per cent vs. 20 per cent) although they were also more likely to see their overall income as unfair (50 per cent vs. 20 per cent). Statistically, this is explained by the majority of dispatched workers being unsure on this question. The result does, however, point to the complexity of the issue and suggests some other variable(s), such as time spent at their present company, may be important in this regard. Similarly, contract workers also had a more negative response to working hours, with 20 per cent perceiving hours of work being unfair. Contract workers were also less likely to see wages as fair (57 per cent vs. 100 per cent), benefits (58 per cent vs. 75 per cent), contract arrangements (71 per cent vs. 100 per cent), promotion opportunities (65 per cent vs. 100 per cent) and training arrangements (65 per cent vs. 100 per cent). These different responses from the two groups of employees demonstrate that generally dispatched workers were happier with their overall income, working hours and contractual arrangements than their contract employee counterparts.

The age profile of employees also appeared to be an important demographic variable in considering the fairness of the distribution of rewards. Older employees between 35 and 45 years of age as well as those above 45 years were generally more likely to perceive wages and benefits as fair compared to their younger colleagues below 35 years. There was, however, some variation in these findings. Older workers, namely, those above 45 years of age, were more likely to perceive wages, contracts and promotions as fair compared to younger workers. These older workers were, however, more likely to perceive overall income as unfair. Workers aged between 35 and 45 years saw the arrangement of working hours in a more negative light but had relatively higher perceptions of fairness with regard to other benefits and training opportunities. Overall, fewer younger employees (those under 35 years of age) saw benefits, promotion and training opportunities as fair, although they were more likely to perceive contract arrangements as fair.

Gender differences in fairness perceptions of current wages and working conditions were reasonably consistent, with more male workers perceiving overall income, working hours, wages, other benefits and training opportunities as fair compared to women employees. In contrast, more female workers perceived contract arrangements and promotion opportunities as fair. Working hours per day presented a major problem for female workers, with only 1 per cent of women employees perceiving these hours as fair. This compares with 37 per cent of male counterparts who perceived their daily hours of work as fair. The discrepancy in this regard reflects the overall family responsibilities carried by women workers and the difficulties they face in achieving an equitable work-life balance.

Employees' education is another demographic variable that may influence perceptions of fairness. Whilst in this study the differences between workers who have tertiary education and those who do not are quite small, the overall picture indicates that more educated workers were less satisfied with wages and conditions of work, with the exception of daily working hours. In this latter case, the difference was small, although it should be noted that 22 per cent of employees without tertiary qualifications thought the daily working hours were unfair compared to 0 per cent for those with tertiary qualifications. This may indicate different working hours for these two groups. These findings also suggest that employees with higher education qualifications might make higher demands for wages and other working conditions given their educational qualifications, their wish for higher social status and the skills shortages.

One important differentiator between workers in China is whether they hold a local *hukou* or residential certificate in the city or region in which they are working. This is important as it will affect their family life, their children's schooling and the availability of various insurances. In short, those without a local *hukou* are considered as migrant workers with commensurate inferior conditions in most aspects of work and daily life. This attitude proved to be the case in this study. Perceptions of fairness among workers holding a local *hukou* was generally higher than among migrant workers. This was the case for wages, other benefits, and contract and training arrangements. Workers with an urban citizenship were also more likely to perceive a fair distribution of wages and other benefits than were workers with rural citizenship. Given the unequal treatment between local and migrant workers, it was surprising to see workers without a local *hukou* perceiving greater fairness in the distribution of overall income and promotional opportunities than those with a local *hukou*. These differences were also noticeable among rural citizens who were more likely to perceive higher levels of fairness in overall income and promotional opportunities, suggesting that these workers' income reference point may be outside the city in which they are working.

Another potential demographic differentiator is whether employees possess professional or occupational certification. Workers with such qualifications were more likely to perceive wages and training arrangements to be fair, although they were less likely to perceive overall income level, other benefits, contract arrangement and promotion opportunities as fair in comparison with workers without professional certification. As illustrated earlier, workers with higher levels of education may assess their current rewards as unfair given their education; likewise, professionally certified employees may maintain that they deserve better treatment given their qualifications and social status.

A further variable to be considered here is the nature and structure of the enterprise in which employees work. As mentioned earlier in this book, our sample of employees is drawn from four types of enterprises: state-owned (SOEs), domestic-private (DPEs), foreign-invested (FIEs) and joint-stock companies (JSCs). Workers in SOEs generally perceived wages, other benefits, and contract and training arrangements as fair, but were less likely to perceive overall income and promotion opportunities the same way. Workers in DPEs perceived contract arrangements, promotion and training opportunities as fair, but were less complimentary about overall income, working hours, wages and other benefits. Workers in FIEs displayed similar perceptions to workers in DPEs, but significantly more FIE workers saw working hours per day as fair (34 per cent and 1 per cent, respectively). Given that this difference was also reflected in comparisons with SOEs and JSCs, it appears that for FIEs working hours in these enterprises may reflect the practices of the foreign company. A higher percentage of workers in JSCs perceived overall income, wages, other benefits, contract arrangements, promotion and training opportunities as fair compared to employees in the other business forms. Although a smaller number of workers were represented in JSCs, it was clear that these workers were more positive about enterprise changes arising from economic reform than their counterparts elsewhere. For these workers, the market-focused reforms provided better pay and working conditions through the linking of individual rewards with firm performance. Workers in FIEs and DPEs have also benefited through better conditions in recent years, although many workers in SOEs might feel that they have missed out more recently on the benefits of the reform process. In this latter case, whilst there has been a strong emphasis on job security, there have been fewer incentives for employees to work hard through reward schemes such as performance-based pay systems.

Interactional fairness

As indicated in Table 5.1 and as discussed earlier in this chapter, another important form of fairness or justice is employees' perceptions of how fairly supervisors support and treat them. In the survey, we asked several questions that related to this interactional fairness, including whether workers felt that they could participate in workplace decision-making and whether their supervisor would listen and discuss job-related issues with them. These are important questions as such fairness validates the organizational standing of workers and, in many cases, leads them to think more highly of management and the enterprise. Whilst workers in both regions were very positive towards their supervisors, more employees in the north (83 per cent) were likely to rate supervisors as fair compared to employees in the south (76 per cent). This difference may have resulted from employees being closer to the macro-policy decision-making centre (Beijing) and where supervisors could explain such changes more directly than their southern counterparts. Similarly, employees aged between 35 and 45 years, those with lower education levels, those with local *hukou* status, those with professional certification and those working in SOEs and JSCs were generally found to assess the interactions with their supervisor as fairer than was the case with their relevant counterparts. Whilst many of these differences were expected, it was interesting to find that the possession of professional certification led to more workers assessing supervisor interactions as fair than having superior educational qualifications. Clearly, supervisors will seek advice and interact more openly with workers they see as having relevant qualifications and experience for the job. Results are presented in Tables 5.2 and 5.3.

Employee satisfaction

Employee satisfaction with their job and working conditions varied considerably in this study and this was most pronounced in terms of location. Only 42 per cent of workers in the north were satisfied with their job and working conditions compared to 87 per cent in the south. More workers in the north were also not satisfied with their job (11 per cent) compared to their southern counterparts (2 per cent). Results are presented in Table 5.2. As was pointed out earlier, such differences may have more to do with northern employees' comparative frame of reference than anything inherent in their present job. Nevertheless, forms of employment and demographic variables may help to explain some of these differences.

Contract workers were generally more satisfied (83 per cent) than dispatched workers (60 per cent). Dispatched workers are often migrant workers and whilst their wages and working conditions are better than their previous jobs (e.g. farmers or other irregular jobs), they do not enjoy the same level of rewards received by contract workers. Moreover, dispatched workers lack job security and often find it difficult to develop a sense of belonging to their current organization. In contrast, whilst enjoying better wages and conditions of work than dispatched workers, formal contract workers often feel negative towards their current pay and working conditions (see Table 5.3). In other words, contract workers' frame of reference is not based on dispatched workers, but rather on other contract workers with whom they work or come into contact with, such as family or friends.

As Table 5.3 illustrates, two demographic variables suggest some important differences in satisfaction levels: education and enterprise type. Those without tertiary qualifications generally appeared more satisfied (89 per cent) than workers with tertiary qualifications (77 per cent), indicating their general satisfaction with most of the components of their work and rewards. Likewise, employees of JSCs also indicated significantly higher levels of satisfaction with their job and conditions of work (81 per cent) than employees working in SOEs, DPEs and FIEs. Employees in SOEs had the lowest ratings in this regard (52 per cent). These levels of satisfaction appear to be based on objective criteria given that employees of JSCs were significantly more satisfied with wages and most of the benefits than workers in other types of enterprises.

Conclusion

This chapter explored the issue of employee fairness or justice at the enterprise level following a period of major economic reform. The macroeconomic reform agenda impacted significantly on the nature of the enterprise and the adoption of 'modern management' systems with the major emphasis on efficiency, productivity and performance-based rewards. After more than four decades of this market-oriented economic reform, workers have generally transitioned well from the former equality-based distribution system to an equity-based system. There appears to be a strong alignment between the reform agenda and employees' expectations. Workers appear to understand that the improved economic performance of firms can lead to better pay and benefits for them, although many workers have negative views of the impact on overall income, workload and working hours, and some other benefits. Regional differences, in this case between cities in the north and the south, reflect some of these views and highlight the varied impact of macro-policy changes on enterprise-level management practices.

The findings of this chapter present a diverse set of views and impacts among workers in different locations (north and south), employment forms (contract status), demographic characteristics (age, gender, education, *hukou* status and professional certification) and enterprise structure. Generally speaking, employees in the south (Hunan and Guangdong) were significantly more satisfied with their job and employment conditions than those in the north (Beijing and Hebei). This finding, as noted, extended to employees' assessment of the fairness of changes to the organization of work and the influence of those changes to their working lives. The employment conditions of formal contract workers were better than for dispatched workers, but given their different historical and social background, dispatched workers were happier with their overall income, working hours and contractual arrangements in comparison with formal contract workers. As we discussed earlier, many dispatched workers are also migrant workers and their experiences as migrant workers may lead them to making different comparisons in assessing their wages and conditions. Likewise, contract workers' comparisons are most likely to refer to other contract workers who may well be earning as much or more.

Location and forms of employment were not the only differentiators in employees' perceptions of fairness. As demonstrated in this chapter, a number of employee demographic factors were relevant in this regard. Education and professional qualifications did not prove to be significant differentiators. Surprisingly, however, workers with lower education and professional certification tended to be more satisfied and perceived working conditions as fairer compared to their more highly qualified counterparts. Again, such perceptions are likely to be strongly influenced by these workers' perceived 'value' and 'social status'. Likewise, whilst gender was not a strong differentiator, male workers were generally more satisfied with the current pay and working conditions compared with female workers. This difference was most noticeable in the case of working hours where many women face the daily difficulty of balancing work and family responsibilities.

Younger workers (under 35 years) were less satisfied with their current income and working conditions compared to older workers (those aged 35 years and older). This partly explains the high turnover rate in more recent years amongst young workers who seek jobs paying higher wages (Jiang, 2018). Perhaps the most striking difference is the comparison between workers with a local *hukou* and those without such a residential pass. The overall level of satisfaction among the workers with a local *hukou*, particularly with those with urban citizenship, is much higher than the migrant workers with rural *hukou* status. Given the unequal treatment between local/urban and migrant/rural workers, such as the payment of the five insurances, the rural and urban divide clearly remains an issue in the Chinese labour market.

The findings also reveal a further difference with regard to enterprise structure or ownership matters. Workers in JSCs were more positive with regard to recent changes. This response is understandable given the benefits of market economic reform for the employees of these firms, resulting in better pay and working conditions, notwithstanding the dependency of wages on firm performance. Many workers in FIEs and DPEs have also gained better conditions in recent years, aided in part by a more competitive and diverse labour market. In contrast, workers in SOEs have not experienced significant reform in recent years, and whilst reforms have provided them with a degree of job security, they have also restricted the use of incentives such as performance-based pay. In short, these findings reflect a firm's willingness to adopt a progressive reform agenda (both externally and internally driven), including modern management and human resource practices, which will lead to increased productivity and competitiveness and thus improved pay and working conditions. In contrast, many of the SOEs have become or are in danger of becoming uncompetitive.

The market-oriented economic reform in recent years has provided the basis for improving firm competitiveness through the adoption of modern management systems. At the firm level, this would clearly impact on workers through the linking of worker rewards to productivity and performance. Consequently, many changes have occurred related to wages, working conditions and overall employee benefits, and satisfaction. The findings presented in this chapter illustrate that workers' overall responses towards policy and organizational change are generally positive though overall income and daily working hours are perceived rather negatively. Importantly, it is evident that some clear regional differences and differences among different types of workers and enterprises exist. In many ways, the initial changes were difficult for workers to accept (see Zhu, Webber and Benson, 2010), although after nearly four decades of economic reform, workers appear to have accepted the equity-based distribution principle and believe that as long as they are hardworking and committed, they will gain from the benefits of the reform agenda. This is not, however, a universally accepted view and important perceptual differences have been identified. Further reform to address these inequality issues will be necessary to develop a fairer and sustainable society. The following chapter will extend this analysis by exploring general well-being among workers.

6 Well-being and satisfaction among workers

Introduction

As indicated in the previous chapter, the workers surveyed in the present study generally perceived their workplaces to be fair and experienced relatively high levels of satisfaction with their employment during the post-reform process in China. These findings, however, varied depending on location and a range of worker and enterprise factors. This chapter will investigate these perceptions in greater detail by focusing on workers' overall well-being and satisfaction with their jobs. We will explore a number of attitudinal and psychological impacts of work that are beyond the work and employment conditions normally considered. Five important aspects of the effects of work will be analyzed: employee health, general satisfaction with the nature of the job, workload and opportunities, support from supervisors and co-workers, and organizational commitment. The impacts may be related to pay and working conditions but more generally represent the complexities of the work and organizational environment. In many cases, the basis for certain responses relies on attitudinal and perceptual views and can be used as a predictor of the long-term physical and psychological health of workers and the labour force more generally. This finding, in turn, will provide an indication of the success of the reform agenda and the likely long-term outcomes.

The chapter commences with a discussion on these physical and psychological aspects of work. These are complex issues and are often intertwined with the inherent nature and physical pressures of work. Wherever possible, the chapter will adopt well-accepted measures of these variables. The next section presents a short discussion of the data and the measures used. The chapter then presents and discusses the findings of this research. As was the case in Chapter 5, the data will be broken down by the various worker and organizational characteristics. The chapter concludes by outlining the importance of the findings for the well-being of workers and the potential impact on the overall reform agenda.

Physical and psychological aspects of work

In China, macro-economic reform has been wide ranging and has significantly affected managers and workers, the structure of the enterprise, labour and employment laws, and the way workers are recruited, managed and incentivized (Benson and Zhu, 1999; Warner, 2011). These issues were discussed in Chapter 2. In this chapter, we want to ascertain how the reform at the enterprise level has impacted on workers' health and general well-being. Younger workers will, of course, have experienced less of these changes compared to their older counterparts, and this can be seen in the breakdown of the findings by age categories. Our analysis will thus be able to advance some tentative predictions for the impact and future success of the reform process.

Employee health is a critical outcome of a range of factors, not all of which are related to work. There are a number of ways to assess workers' health, although generally workers' perceptions of their overall health, as well as their relative perceptions of their health compared to similar workers of the same age, provide a useful starting point. The transition from a central command system to a socialist-market approach, albeit with 'Chinese characteristics' (Warner, 2011), means that higher job stress levels are likely as workers adjust to new ways of working, adopt new technologies and attempt to meet the new production and efficiency targets (Benson and Zhu, 1999). In order to go deeper into the psychological aspects of workers' health, the present analysis will examine whether workers are experiencing various degrees of job stress and whether this is a major problem associated with the reform process at the micro-economic level.

Job stress is defined in various ways, although it is generally considered to occur when an employee is not able to fulfil the demands of the job (House, 1981). Job stress can be caused by a number of factors, such as unclear job responsibilities, work overload, inadequate resources and workplace conflict (Price, 1997), and can lead to workers adopting negative attitudes towards the enterprise, supervisors or co-workers, as well as behavioural outcomes, both within and outside work (Workplace Testing, 2019). There are important antecedents of job stress that arise partially or solely from outside the workplace, such as family-work conflict (Chen, 2011), although much of the stress associated with the job is work related (Price, 1997). The stress includes aspects such as the emotional input required in a job (Jung and Yoon, 2014). There are also important outcomes from high levels of job stress, including reduced work performance, diminished social relationships, higher absenteeism, poor levels of job satisfaction and organizational commitment, and a higher willingness to quit (Harshana, 2018). Clearly, the physical and psychological health of workers is critical to the success of enterprises.

Satisfaction with work was discussed in Chapter 5. In that chapter, we focused on overall satisfaction with work and conditions of employment.

In this chapter, we will extend this analysis by focusing on four attributes of work: tasks, accountabilities, responsibilities and participation in management. These are important aspects of work that are directly linked to enterprise reform in HRM (Storey, 1995). Under modern HRM practices, each worker is given a series of tasks to perform. This set of tasks is typically contained in a job description and each worker will be assessed in a performance review against that job description and each individual task. Workers who perform well in the job may be paid a performance-related bonus. This practice is different from that of the past in Chinese enterprises and, as discussed in Chapter 5, goes to the core of the equity versus equality debate.

Accountability and responsibility are important aspects of strategic HRM where the aim is to align the work of line managers and employees with the strategic aims of the organization (Storey, 1995; Boxall and Purcell, 2003). Workers are now more likely to have the freedom to make some decisions and plan their daily activities where possible, but running parallel to this is the higher level of responsibility that each worker is expected to assume. Yet, in transitionary periods not all employees embrace such an approach and as a consequence may prefer the past ways of working. This may also be related to the level of communication with and participation in management. Where workers have a voice in the decisions affecting their work, it is more likely that they will take ownership of the resultant outcomes and be more satisfied with their job (Spector, 1997).

Another important employment transition due to the reform process in China relates to employees' workloads and job opportunities. Under the planned economy, jobs were closely aligned with government-set targets, employees were assigned tasks and were generally rewarded equally. As pointed out above, under the current market-oriented system, workers have a series of tasks to perform and targets to meet. These targets can be more open-ended than those in the past and exceeding such targets can result in financial rewards (Benson, Debroux and Yuasa, 1998). However, workloads can become excessive, at least in comparison with the past.

Equally, whilst many jobs are routine, there are now greater opportunities for workers to take on a variety of tasks through teamwork, multi-skilling, the introduction of new technologies and the varied demands of international markets (Benson, Debroux, Yuasa and Zhu, 2000). Thus, whether the job is routine or has variety may well be an important difference and a source of opportunity or, if routine in nature, a constraint on future promotion and advancement opportunities. If the job is routine in nature, it is likely that a higher level of job control is exercised and if this is the case, opportunities will be reduced. If, however, there is a low level of job control where workers have variety in the work they do and can make decisions about how they do this work, it should follow that potential opportunities will arise.

Relationships at work are an important factor affecting workers' job satisfaction (Spector, 1997). The reform process in China has led to new and more individualistic ways of working and diminishing opportunities for workers to socialize through company-sponsored housing, recreation and social organizations. It would be expected that these aspects may impact on the level of co-worker support in the workplace. Equally, supervisors in the new era may well be more relaxed about direct control and be more focused on performance. As a consequence, supervisors may see their primary role as assisting their subordinates to achieve the targets, which will reflect favourably on their supervisory capabilities. In this case, supervisor support may be stronger than in the past.

Many of the issues discussed above will impact, either positively or negatively, on employees' level of organizational commitment, and commitment will have important consequences for organizations (Steers, 1977; Meyer and Allen, 1997). Organizational commitment is essentially loyalty to an organization (Price, 1997, p. 335) and is commonly defined as 'the strength of an individual's identification with and involvement in a particular organization' (Porter, Steers, Mowday and Boulian, 1974: 604). Commitment encompasses three aspects: a 'belief in and an acceptance of the organizations' goals and values', 'a willingness to exert considerable effort', and a 'desire to maintain organizational membership' (Porter, Steers, Mowday and Boulian, 1974, p. 604). These features cover both attitudinal and behavioural commitment. Employees' identification with the organization's goals and values is a measure of attitudinal commitment, whilst employees' desire to maintain organizational membership is a measure of behavioural commitment (Coopey and Hartley, 1991; Iverson, 1996; Mowday, Porter and Steers, 1982). We will refer to this last aspect as an employee's willingness to quit.

The above discussion sets the framework for this chapter. These five factors, which are outlined in Table 6.1, provide a way of addressing the question of how the extension of the macro-economic reform agenda to enterprises has impacted on workers' well-being, especially their health, the work they undertake, the key relationships at the workplace and the effect on their attitudinal and behavioural commitment. Whilst these are different measures of work satisfaction compared to those used in Chapter 5, together they provide a good assessment of how changes in labour policies and the organization of work have influenced the way enterprises and workers have responded and reacted to the Chinese reform agenda.

Data

In attempting to understand how macro-economic reform has impacted on the well-being and satisfaction of workers, this chapter delves more deeply into how workers feel, cope with and individually respond to significant changes in work and employment over a long period of time. Five themes will underpin the analysis and the corresponding broad questions utilized in the survey are detailed in Table 6.1. The wider research methodology used to gather this data was discussed in Chapter 1. The survey included a mix of

Table 6.1 Research themes and worker survey questions

Research themes	Survey questions
Employees' health	• How would you rate your general health? • How would you assess your general health compared to other workers of your own age (either in your company or other companies) that you know? • Job stress: 7-item scale developed by House (1981).
Employees' work	• How satisfied are you with your current work: tasks, accountabilities, responsibilities, participation in management? • Was your work worse or better five years ago: tasks, accountabilities, responsibilities, participation in management?
Employees' work load and opportunities	• Work overload: 4-item scale developed by Price and Mueller (1981) and Iverson (1992). • Routinization: 3-item scale developed by Price and Mueller (1981). • Job control: 4-item scale developed by Frese, King, Soose and Zempel (1996).
Supervisor and co-worker support	• Supervisor support: 5-item scale developed by Michaels and Spector (1982). • Co-worker support: 3-item scale developed by House (1981).
Employee Commitment	• Organizational commitment: 9-item scale developed by Porter, Steers, Mowday and Boulian (1974). • Willingness to quit: 2-item scale developed by Porter, Steers, Mowday and Boulian (1974).

Source: Worker survey.

direct questions and well-established scales that addressed workers' general and relative health, and the level of job stress; satisfaction with work in terms of tasks, accountabilities, responsibilities and participation in management, and whether this was better or worse five years ago; workloads and limitations on work opportunities due to the routine nature of the job or the level of managerial control; supervisor and co-worker support; and the commitment of employees as measured by organizational commitment and a willingness to quit.

Apart from a small number of single item questions (general and relative health, present and past satisfaction with tasks, accountabilities, responsibilities and participation in management), the remaining variables were measured by established scales. The broad reliability of the scales can be ascertained by the alpha coefficient (Cronbach, 1951). The alpha coefficient measures the reliability or internal consistency of the items making up a scale; that is, how well the scale, as a whole, measures what it purports to measure. The closer the value of the coefficient is to 1, the more reliable the scale. These values are reported below for each scale and generally demonstrate a high degree of reliability. A five-point Likert scale was used for each scale (1 = strongly disagree; 5 = strongly agree), and scale scores were calculated by averaging the responses to the items. Reverse coding was used where required. Table 6.5 provides the results for these scale variables. In order to maintain consistency and to facilitate comparisons with tables in this and other chapters, the results are broken into three categories: low (1.0 to 2.5), unsure (more than 2.5 but less than 3.5) and high (3.5 to 5.0). The scales used in the analysis for this chapter are as follow:

Stress: Job stress was measured using seven items adapted from House's (1981) scale. The seven items were: my job tends to directly affect my health; I work under a great deal of tension; I have felt fidgety or nervous as a result of my job; if I had a different job, my health would probably improve; problems associated with my job have kept me awake at night; I have felt nervous before attending meetings in the company; and I often 'take my job home with me' in the sense that I think about my job when doing other things. The alpha coefficient for this scale was .884, whilst the mean and standard deviation were 2.21 and 0.86, respectively.

Work overload: Work overload was measured using four items from the scale developed by Price and Mueller (1981) and modified by Iverson (1992). The four items were: my job requires me to work too fast, my job leaves me with little time to get everything done, my job requires me to work very hard (physically or mentally) and I often have to work overtime. The alpha coefficient for this scale was .871, whilst the mean and standard deviation were 2.52 and 1.03, respectively.

Routinization: The degree to which work was routine was measured by a 3-item scale developed by Price and Mueller (1981). The three items were: my job has variety, the duties in my job are repetitive (i.e. I have to do the same thing over and over) and I have the opportunity to do a number of different things in my job. The alpha coefficient for this scale was .627, whilst the mean and standard deviation were 2.68 and 0.95, respectively.

Job control: Job control was measured by the 4-item scale developed by Frese et al. (1996). The four items were: I can make many decisions concerning my job, I can determine how to do my work, I can plan and arrange my work on my own and I can fully participate in decisions made by my supervisor. The alpha coefficient for this scale was .861, whilst the mean and standard deviation were 2.47 and 1.03, respectively.

Supervisor support: Support from the supervisor was measured by five items adapted from Michaels and Spector (1982). The five items were:

my supervisor is willing to listen to work-related problems, I feel free to discuss job-related problems with my supervisor, I am comfortable expressing my feelings to my supervisor, my supervisor can be relied on when things get difficult at work and my supervisor is very concerned about the welfare of those under him/her. The alpha coefficient for this scale was .919, whilst the mean and standard deviation were 3.08 and 1.01, respectively.

Co-worker support: Support from co-workers was measure by the 3-item scale developed by House (1981). The three items were: my peers can be relied upon when things get difficult on my job, my peers are willing to listen to job-related problems and my peers are helpful to me in getting my job done. The alpha coefficient for this scale was .733, whilst the mean and standard deviation were 3.24 and 0.98, respectively.

Organizational commitment: Commitment to the organization was measured by the 9-item scale developed by Porter et al. (1974) and Mowday, Steers and Porter (1979). The nine items were: I am willing to put in a great deal of effort beyond that normally required to help the company be successful, I promote the company to my friends as a great place to work, I would accept almost any type of work to keep working for this company, I am proud to tell others that I work for this company, the company inspires the very best in me in the way of job performance, I am extremely pleased that I chose to work for this company over the others I was considering at the time, I really care about the future of this company, for me this company is the best place to work and I find my values and that of the company very similar. The alpha coefficient for this scale was .941, whilst the mean and standard deviation were 2.80 and 0.94, respectively.

Willingness to quit: Willingness to quit was measured by the 2-item scale developed by Porter et al. (1974). The two items were: there is not much to be gained from working for this company for ever, and it would take very little for me to change employers. The alpha coefficient for this scale was .674, whilst the mean and standard deviation were 2.08 and 0.95, respectively.

As in early chapters, the analysis takes into account the diversity of workers surveyed in terms of location (northern China and southern China), employment type (contract arrangement), personal characteristics (age, gender, educational qualifications and professional/occupational certification), household registration (urban or rural, local or migrant) and enterprise structure. Details of these variables were presented in Chapter 1 (see Table 1.2), whilst Chapter 5 provided the rationale for taking such variables into account in the analysis. In short, the following analysis will break down the results by dispatched and contract workers, age group, gender, education, local *hukou* status, urban and rural citizens, professional certification and enterprise ownership. Results are shown in Tables 6.2–6.5.

Table 6.2 Employees' general and relative health (%)

	General health			Relative health		
	Good	Unsure	Poor	Better	Unsure	Worse
All workers	75	23	1	47	48	5
Enterprise location						
North	78	21	1	50	48	2
South	73	25	1	45	47	8
Worker type						
Dispatched workers	62	37	1	47	45	8
Contract workers	77	22	1	49	47	4
Age						
<35 years old	80	19	1	49	45	6
35–45	81	17	3	48	46	6
>45 years old	74	26	0	45	42	3
Gender						
Male	76	23	1	50	45	5
Female	75	24	1	45	50	5
Education						
Tertiary and above	71	28	1	42	56	2
Below tertiary	81	18	1	54	42	4
Local Hukou status						
Yes	75	24	1	44	50	6
No	76	22	2	53	44	3
Urban/rural citizen						
Urban	74	24	2	44	51	5
Rural	79	20	1	55	41	4
Certification						
Yes	75	24	1	50	45	5
No	76	22	2	46	49	5
Enterprise ownership						
SOEs	74	25	1	44	51	5
DPEs	76	22	2	47	45	8
FIEs	74	25	1	53	46	1
JSCs	83	17	0	51	43	6

Source: Worker survey.

Table 6.3 Employees' current satisfaction with work (%)

	Tasks			Accountabilities			Responsibilities			Participation		
	Dissatisfied	It's all right	Satisfied	Dissatisfied	It's all right	Satisfied	Dissa-tisfied	It's all right	Satisfied	Dissati-sfied	It's all right	Satisf-ed
All workers	43	57	0	33	58	9	37	58	5	60	36	4
Enterprise location												
North	46	54	0	36	56	8	38	57	5	58	38	4
South	41	59	0	31	59	10	36	58	6	62	34	4
Worker type												
Dispatched workers	53	47	0	41	51	8	36	59	5	65	32	3
Contract workers	43	57	0	32	58	10	37	57	6	60	36	4
Age												
<35 years old	45	55	0	36	56	9	37	57	5	62	34	4
35–45	44	56	0	31	58	11	42	52	6	60	37	3
>45 years old	34	66	0	24	67	10	24	70	6	50	45	5
Gender												
Male	43	57	0	35	55	10	37	57	6	59	37	4
Female	44	56	0	31	60	9	37	58	5	61	35	4
Education												
Tertiary and above	39	61	0	32	57	12	36	57	7	59	34	6
Below tertiary	47	53	0	35	58	7	38	57	5	61	37	2

(Continued)

Table 6.3 (Continued)

	Tasks			Accountabilities			Responsibilities			Participation		
	Dissatisfied	It's all right	Satisfied	Dissatisfied	It's all right	Satisfied	Dissatisfied	It's all right	Satisfied	Dissatisfied	It's all right	Satisfied
Local Hukou status												
Yes	44	56	0	32	58	10	35	59	6	58	38	4
No	43	57	0	36	56	8	40	55	5	63	34	3
Urban/rural citizen												
Urban	42	58	0	32	58	10	35	60	5	60	36	4
Rural	46	54	0	35	56	9	40	53	7	60	36	4
Certification												
Yes	40	60	0	29	59	12	35	59	6	55	40	5
No	47	53	0	38	55	7	39	56	5	66	31	3
Enterprise ownership												
SOEs	45	55	0	36	55	9	41	54	5	62	33	5
DPEs	37	63	0	26	63	11	29	65	6	52	44	4
FIEs	47	53	0	35	55	9	41	53	6	67	29	4
JSCs	51	49	0	42	51	8	47	49	4	72	26	2

Source: Worker survey.

Table 6.4 Employees' satisfaction with work five years ago relative to the present (%)

	Tasks			Accountabilities			Responsibilities			Participation		
	Worse	Same	Better	Worse	Same	Better	Worse	Same	Better	Worse	Same	Better
All workers	54	39	7	51	43	6	52	40	8	57	35	7
Enterprise location												
North	55	41	4	50	44	6	55	37	8	58	34	8
South	53	37	10	52	42	6	50	43	7	57	36	7
Worker type												
Dispatched workers	50	44	6	56	31	13	50	44	6	56	31	13
Contract workers	55	38	7	51	44	5	53	39	8	58	36	6
Age												
<35 years old	52	43	5	55	39	6	51	37	12	58	33	10
35–45	55	36	9	49	47	4	50	44	6	57	38	5
>45 years old	56	38	6	48	44	8	59	37	4	59	37	4
Gender												
Male	55	37	8	51	42	7	51	41	8	54	37	9
Female	52	41	7	50	44	6	54	38	8	62	33	5
Education												
Tertiary and above	53	41	6	52	41	7	50	41	9	53	39	8
Below tertiary	55	38	7	50	44	6	54	39	7	61	32	7
Local Hukou status												
Yes	54	39	7	50	43	7	53	40	7	57	35	8

(Continued)

Table 6.4 (Continued)

	Tasks			Accountabilities			Responsibilities			Participation		
	Worse	Same	Better	Worse	Same	Better	Worse	Same	Better	Worse	Same	Better
No	53	39	8	54	43	3	52	41	7	60	35	5
Urban/rural citizen												
Urban	55	38	7	50	43	7	53	38	9	57	35	8
Rural	46	44	10	54	42	4	49	45	6	58	38	4
Certification												
Yes	54	37	9	52	41	7	52	40	8	54	38	9
No	54	41	5	50	45	5	54	39	7	63	32	5
Enterprise ownership												
SOEs	59	32	9	48	42	10	52	38	10	53	37	10
DPEs	45	48	7	46	51	3	47	44	9	56	39	5
FIEs	56	37	7	65	29	6	59	35	6	72	23	5
JSCs	62	38	0	46	54	0	62	38	0	54	46	0

Source: Worker survey.

Table 6.5 Employees' well-being and satisfaction (%)

	Job stress			Work overload			Routinization			Job control		
	Low	*Unsure*	*High*	*Low*	*Unsure*	*High*	*Low*	*Unsure*	*High*	*Low*	*Unsure*	*High*
All workers	60	33	7	49	29	22	37	42	21	51	28	21
Enterprise location												
North	89	10	1	80	19	1	70	28	2	77	22	1
South	32	56	12	20	38	42	6	55	39	25	35	40
Worker type												
Dispatched workers	23	52	26	17	32	51	12	60	28	35	32	33
Contract workers	63	33	4	53	28	19	40	40	20	52	28	20
Age												
<35 years old	60	33	7	53	26	21	40	42	18	52	28	20
35–45	60	34	6	45	32	23	37	41	22	49	29	22
>45 years old	54	40	6	36	41	23	23	45	32	40	33	27
Gender												
Male	48	42	10	39	29	32	32	43	25	45	29	26
Female	72	25	3	61	29	10	44	40	16	58	28	14
Education												
Tertiary and above	61	31	8	50	27	23	41	41	18	53	27	20
Below tertiary	57	37	6	49	31	20	34	43	23	48	31	21
Local Hukou status												
Yes	61	32	7	52	28	20	43	39	18	52	29	19
No	57	38	5	45	30	25	30	45	25	48	29	23
Urban/rural citizen												

(*Continued*)

Table 6.5 (continued)

	Job stress			Work overload			Routinization			Job control		
	Low	Unsure	High	Low	Unsure	High	Low	Unsure	High	Low	Unsure	High
Urban	62	32	6	51	29	20	38	42	20	51	28	21
Rural	54	39	7	47	29	24	35	42	23	50	30	20
Certification												
Yes	53	40	7	44	32	24	31	43	26	44	31	25
No	65	28	7	54	26	20	44	40	16	56	27	17
Enterprise ownership												
SOEs	59	36	5	49	34	17	35	40	25	51	30	19
DPEs	60	32	8	50	24	26	44	39	17	56	20	24
FIEs	65	31	4	57	28	15	38	50	12	50	32	18
JSCs	27	59	14	32	47	21	10	45	45	23	42	35

	Supervisor support			Co-worker support			Employee commitment			Willingness to quit		
	Low	Unsure	High	Low	Unsure	High	Low	Unsure	High	Low	Unsure	High
All workers	29	29	42	22	29	49	36	39	25	64	28	8
Enterprise location												
North	58	38	4	44	42	14	65	33	2	88	11	0
South	1	20	79	1	16	83	7	45	48	40	44	16
Worker type												
Dispatched workers	5	23	72	5	13	82	5	40	55	45	45	10
Contract workers	32	29	39	24	30	46	38	39	23	64	27	9
Age												
<35 years old	31	28	41	23	28	49	37	39	24	63	28	9
35–45	28	30	42	24	28	48	35	38	27	65	26	9

>45 years old	17	33	50	15	32	53	23	44	33	50	42	8
Gender												
Male	25	27	48	20	26	54	31	42	27	58	32	10
Female	34	32	34	26	31	43	41	36	23	68	26	6
Education												
Tertiary and above	30	30	40	25	31	44	39	38	23	68	26	6
Below tertiary	28	28	44	20	26	54	32	40	28	57	33	10
Local Hukou status												
Yes	34	27	39	27	31	43	42	37	21	66	28	6
No	23	31	46	17	25	58	26	43	31	58	30	12
Urban/rural citizen												
Urban	30	29	41	24	30	46	38	38	24	65	28	7
Rural	29	28	43	20	25	55	30	40	30	57	31	12
Certification												
Yes	24	28	48	20	26	54	30	40	30	62	31	7
No	34	29	37	24	31	45	41	39	20	62	27	11
Enterprise ownership												
SOEs	27	27	46	23	30	47	39	32	29	63	29	8
DPEs	34	29	37	26	24	50	28	42	20	65	27	8
FIEs	32	31	37	19	32	49	37	43	20	63	29	8
JSCs	2	25	73	1	25	74	3	42	55	35	48	17

Source: Worker survey.

Worker well-being and satisfaction with work

Employees' health

Workers were asked how they would rate their general health. Three-quarters of respondents felt their health was generally good or very good (75 per cent). This result represents a relatively high proportion of workers although 23 per cent were unsure, rating their health as neither good nor bad. Only 1 per cent felt their general health was quite poor or poor. These findings were quite consistent across the various categories of workers, although some variations are worth noting. Workers from the north felt they were more healthy (78 per cent compared to 73 per cent in the south), as did contract workers (77 per cent compared to 62 per cent of dispatched workers), younger workers (80 per cent under 45 years compared to 74 per cent over 45 years of age), those without tertiary qualifications (81 per cent compared to 71 per cent of tertiary qualified workers) and rural citizens (79 per cent compared to 74 per cent of urban workers). Enterprise ownership did not seem to be a factor, although 83 per cent of Joint stock companies (JSCs) workers reported a good or very good level of general health. This result may, however, be a product of the small number of workers in this category. Importantly, these figures also represent some of the underpinning contextual factors. For example, workers in the north are generally younger, work in tertiary type jobs and are university trained; all factors suggest a healthier population of workers.

Assessment of health can be based on a range of factors which lead to some variations between respondents. We therefore asked workers to assess their general health relative to workers of their own age in their company or another company that they knew. Overall, a little under half of the workers (47 per cent) perceived their health to be better or much better than others that they knew of a similar age. Equally, just under half (48 per cent) also reported their health was neither better nor worse than others. Only 5 per cent felt their general health was worse or much worse. Again, these findings were consistesnt across the various categories of workers and were generally consistent with the results reported above. Slightly higher levels of relative health were reported by workers in the north (50 per cent compared to 45 per cent of workers from the south), younger workers, male employees (50 per cent of male workers compared to 45 per cent of women workers), those qualified below tertiary level, those with no local *hukou* (53 per cent compared to 44 per cent of those workers with local *hukou*), those with rural residency (55 per cent compared to 45 per cent), and professionally qualified and employees of JSCs. Results for both health measures are presented in Table 6.2.

Whilst the above findings tell us something about the general state of health of workers in China, the types of workers surveyed were generally in large enterprises where some protection is afforded through labour laws and enterprise policy and norms. The typical respondents appear to assess their health as good and generally better than others they know of the same age. Yet, with reform comes considerable pressure to adapt to new ways of working, modern technology and more stringent production targets. Does such a transition result in high levels of job stress? Some indication of job stress, or simply the excessive pressures of the job, can be gauged by using the 7-item job stress scale developed by House (1981). Details of this scale can be found in the data section of this chapter and Table 6.1.

The survey revealed that only 7 per cent of workers felt high levels of job stress. The majority (60 per cent) of workers felt little stress at work, although 33 per cent were undecided. This finding is consistent with that discussed in Chapter 5, indicating that many workers were satisfied in their present job. Similarly, the finding supports the overall assessment of workers with respect to their general health. It is, however, difficult to reconcile this result with the finding later in this chapter that in certain areas of their work many workers were not satisfied, although they did recognize that they were less satisfied five years ago.

The workplace can be stressful due to the high expectations and demands of the enterprise, individual managers and supervisors. The effect on workers will depend, however, on a range of worker and enterprise characteristics referred to earlier in this chapter. The location of the enterprise was an important determinant in our survey, with 89 per cent of workers in the north experiencing low levels of stress compared to 32 per cent of workers from the south. This finding is partly a result of the higher concentration of tertiary industry in the north and a higher percentage of male and dispatched workers in the south (see Tables 1.1 and 1.2). Fewer dispatched workers (23 per cent) and male employees (48 per cent) recorded low levels of stress compared to contract or women workers (63 per cent and 72 per cent, respectively). Differences based on the age of workers or educational qualifications were minimal, although those without professional/ occupational accreditation were less likely to feel stressed (65 per cent compared to 53 per cent). This result may be related to the type of work, the level of the job or the possession of tertiary qualifications. As expected, those without local *hukou* status or those who were rural citizens tended to have higher levels of job stress, although these differences were generally not substantial. With the exception of JSCs, the differences in worker stress levels between various ownership models were not significant. Details are present in Table 6.5.

Satisfaction with work

Chapter 5 provided some measure and discussion of employees' overall satisfaction with their jobs and working conditions. Some 65 per cent of workers were found to be satisfied with their jobs, although this was significantly down on the figure of 83 per cent reported a decade earlier by Zhu, Webber and Benson (2010). Importantly, considerable variation in satisfaction was found between workers in the north (42 per cent) and workers in the south (87 per cent). More detailed analysis is provided in that chapter. In this section, we focus on four aspects of the current work role: tasks, accountabilities, responsibilities and participation in management. Our focus can thus be directed towards the key aspects of work rather than be confounded by attitudes towards wages, working conditions and social relations at work. In order to gain an understanding of what these responses mean, we also asked respondents to assess whether these work roles were worse or better five years ago.

These four aspects of work have generally intensified over the past decade or so and have broadened in many organizations worldwide where job descriptions define the tasks to be completed, job responsibilities are carefully detailed and accountabilities specified. As a result, participation in decision-making may have decreased, although this is by no means certain. In this study, the percentage of workers who were satisfied (satisfied and very satisfied) in these four areas was extremely low at 0 per cent, 9 per cent, 5 per cent and 4 per cent, respectively. With the exception of participation in management (36 per cent), the majority of workers responded 'it's all right' (57 per cent, 58 per cent and 58 per cent, respectively) to the other aspects, which illustrates a less than enthusiastic response to how they feel about these aspects of their jobs. These levels of satisfaction, with the exception of participation, are significantly less than the figures reported in Zhu, Webber and Benson (2010) a decade or so earlier when the corresponding levels of satisfaction were 62 per cent, 73 per cent, 69 per cent and 54 per cent, respectively (page 116). Notwithstanding the different sample of workers, it does appear that the continuing micro-economic and enterprise reform has led to many more workers becoming dissatisfied with these aspects of work. The lower levels of satisfaction in these four areas are consistent with the findings reported in Chapter 5 concerning workers' perceived fairness and overall satisfaction with the job and working conditions.

Table 6.3 breaks these findings down by the demographic variables and worker characteristics used earlier in this chapter and in Chapter 5. Workers in the south were slightly more satisfied (or less dissatisfied) with these aspects of their jobs than those from the north with the exception of participation. Contract workers were also slightly more satisfied than dispatched workers with these aspects of the job with the exception of responsibilities. Similarly, older workers (those over 45 years of age) were more satisfied with these aspects of work which, at least in part, reflects some of the improvements in wages and conditions of employment over the years. Gender was not a distinguishing characteristic between workers and their perceptions of work.

Tertiary education did predict higher levels of satisfaction, which was also the case for workers with professional certification. Whilst this finding was consistent across all four job areas, what was surprising, given the opportunities afforded to this group of workers, is that the differences were not more pronounced. One possible reason is that many of the 'highly' qualified workers have higher expectations than are achievable. It may also be the case that growing up in an era of the 'one-child' policy meant that many of this generation had greater expectations of the value of their education and their place in society. It thus comes as a shock for these 'spoilt' children when the reality of full-time work sets in. Whilst purely speculative, anecdotal evidence collected over a number of years in various settings would support such a proposition. Workers with local *hukou* status were slightly more satisfied with these aspects of work, with the exception of tasks. Similarly, workers with urban citizenship were slightly more satisfied than their rural counterparts, with the exception of participation. Enterprise ownership or structure did not appear to generally affect worker satisfaction levels, with the exception of Domestic private enterprises (DPEs) where workers reported significantly higher levels of satisfaction across all four work aspects. This finding is not surprising given the possible opportunities to be found in these enterprises.

The above findings and discussion reveal a reasonably bleak picture with regard to worker satisfaction in the areas of tasks, accountabilities, responsibilities and participation at the time of the survey. As pointed out earlier in this section, the findings demonstrate a general decline from a decade or so earlier (Zhu, Webber and Benson, 2010). One problem in making such a comparison is that we are not comparing the same group of respondents. We therefore asked respondents to this study whether they felt these aspects of the job were worse or better five years ago. The majority of workers (54 per cent, 51 per cent, 52 per cent and 57 per cent for each aspect, respectively) felt that the four aspects of work were worse five years ago. Less than 10 per cent of respondents claimed the aspects were better and a sizeable minority felt things were much the same.

As in workers' current assessment of their satisfaction with these aspects of work, some variations in assessing their past experiences were found when the results were broken down by various demographic and worker characteristics. Workers in the north were a little more pessimistic in their assessments, although workers in the south tended to assess accountabilities as being worse five years ago. Contract workers generally assessed conditions as worse, although dispatched workers tended to report negative experiences with regard to accountabilities. There were some relatively minor variations based on age, although no consistent pattern emerged. Similarly, gender variations were relatively minor, although women workers felt that their participation in management was better than five years ago. There was little difference in perceptions of these work areas based on educational qualifications or professional certification, although those without tertiary qualifications or professional/occupational certification were more likely to claim participation was worse five years ago. Similarly, having local *hukou* status did not demonstrate different attitudes to work, although urban/rural citizenship appeared to be an important explanatory factor. Workers who were urban citizens felt tasks and responsibilities had improved from five years ago, whilst rural citizens felt this was the case with accountabilities. Finally, some differences based on enterprise ownership was also found. Generally, workers in DPEs were less likely to claim that work in all areas was worse five years ago, whilst generally more workers in Foreign invested enterprises (FIEs) felt work was worse five years ago with respect to accountabilities, responsibilities and participation. The findings are presented in Table 6.4.

Employees' workload and opportunities

One of the critical factors in how workers perceive their well-being and level of job satisfaction is the quantity of work allocated, or more precisely whether workers perceive this workload to be an excessive workplace obligation. This perception can be influenced by the nature of the work (routine or complex) and the level of job control (or autonomy) afforded. In order to gain a clear understanding of the influence of these factors, three well-accepted scales (work overload, routinization and job control) were used, details of which are provided in the data section of this chapter.

Nearly half the workers in this study (49 per cent) felt that their workload was not excessive or overly demanding. In contrast, a smaller number (22 per cent) felt that their job was physically or mentally taxing and they had little time to complete their work. Some important differences could be discerned when work overload was broken down by enterprise and worker characteristics. Enterprise location was an important distinguishing factor with 42 per cent of southern workers feeling overloaded compared to only 1 per cent of workers from the north. Similarly, 51 per cent of dispatched workers felt overworked compared to only 19 per cent of regular contract workers. The latter finding is not surprising given the uncertainty facing dispatched workers not only within the job but also in terms of ongoing employment. Nevertheless, the finding that only a small percentage of workers in the north felt overworked may also be a product of the small number of dispatched workers in that region. Male employees were more likely to feel overloaded with work (32 per cent) compared to only 10 per cent of women workers who, however, may be juggling and be responsible for a larger share of the domestic or home work. Workers with occupational or professional certification were also a little more likely to feel overloaded at work, as were those without local *hukou* status. This last point can be explained to some extent by the uncertainty of their 'migrant' status as well as the fact that these workers often do not enjoy benefits such as the various insurance schemes. Workers in DPEs were also more likely to feel overloaded at work. Details are presented in Table 6.5.

Well-being and satisfaction at work clearly can stem from the demands of the job. The scope of the job can also be an influencing factor. Work that is monotonous or routine in nature can also have a profound effect. Some 21 per cent of workers in this study agreed that their work was routine, with a further 42 per cent indicating they were undecided. There were, however, some important differences between the various categories of workers.

Workers in the south were more likely to claim their work was routine (39 per cent) compared to workers in the north (2 per cent). Part of the reason is the higher levels of mass production or manufacturing in the southern region (see Table 1.1); a further reason is the higher number of dispatched workers in the south (see Table 1.2) who are, as suggested in Table 6.5, also more likely to perceive their jobs as routine. Older workers also had similar perceptions, as did male workers, those without tertiary qualifications or local *hukou* status. Surprisingly workers with professional accreditation and workers in JSCs were more likely to classify their work as routine.

The final factor we explored was job control, which refers to workers' ability to plan and make decisions about their jobs. Some 21 per cent of workers in the study rated their job control as high, compared to 51 per cent who rated this aspect of their work as low. Surprisingly, 40 per cent of workers in the south rated their degree of job control as high, compared to only 1 per cent of northern workers. One explanation for this low level of job control in the north may relate to the nature of the tertiary sector where work is typically dependent on others. It is, however, more likely that the result is unduly influenced by the higher proportion of regular contract workers in the north who appear to have less control over their daily working lives. Older and male workers reported high levels of job control, which is to be expected given their experience and probably higher levels of tenure with the enterprise. As would be expected, workers with professional or occupational certification were more likely to perceive higher levels of job control (25 per cent and 17 per cent, respectively), as did workers in JSCs (35 per cent) and DPEs (24 per cent).

Supervisor and co-worker support

Work is designed around the aims and objectives of the employer or enterprise. Thus, job structures, administrative control and responsibilities, work processes and a myriad of other factors contribute to the nature of the job, the outcomes of such a job, and the well-being and satisfaction that workers can derive from that job. One factor that is often neglected, however, relates to the human or social aspects of the job and whether workers feel supported by those for and with whom they work. Supervisor and co-worker support relates to the way the employee and the enterprise interact. For most workers, the support they receive from their supervisors and co-workers define the organization and their jobs. A friendly and supportive work environment was found to be instrumental in developing organization commitment and lowering intention to quit in the case of knowledge workers (Benson and Brown, 2007).

Supervisor support was rated high by 42 per cent of workers, with only 29 per cent rating it as low. Such support included not only matters related to the job but also issues concerning worker welfare. These figures, however, varied by different enterprise and worker characteristics. Workers in the south were more likely to rate supervisors as supportive (79 per cent compared to 4 percent for their northern counterparts), as were dispatched workers (72 per cent compared to 39 per cent for contract workers). As pointed out earlier, this finding may, at least in part, relate to the small number of dispatched workers in the north. Older workers, male employees and those with tertiary qualifications appear to have more positive relationships with their supervisors. This was also the case for workers without local *hukou* status. This finding can be partly explained by the fact that many 'migrant' workers are recruited from the supervisors' home town. In this case, obligation, previous relationships and gratitude become important factors in the worker-supervisor relationship. Workers from SOEs were more likely to report a positive supervisor relationship than were those from DPEs and FIEs. This finding is related, at least in part, to the lower levels of job stress being experienced by this group of workers. Workers in JSCs rated supervisor support as highest, although the small number of workers in this group makes this figure less reliable. Results are presented in Table 6.5.

Nearly half the workers surveyed (49 per cent) reported a high level of co-worker support, which included not only assistance with the job but also listening to job-related problems. Being able to rely on co-workers is an important aspect of most jobs, although perceptions varied significantly between various groups of workers. Those from the north (83 per cent) and dispatched workers (82 per cent) were more likely to report such support, which is understandable given the flexibility in tertiary type work and the more transitory nature of dispatched employment. As mentioned earlier, however, caution must be taken when interpreting these results. Older workers and male employees were more positive in reporting such support, although, unlike supervisory support, those without tertiary qualifications reported a higher level of support from colleagues. It is likely that these workers had more confidence in seeking advice from co-workers rather than discussing work-related problems with supervisors. A similar argument can be made to explain the finding that a higher percentage of those without a local *hukou* (58 per cent) or had rural citizen status (55 per cent) perceived stronger co-worker support. Those with professional or occupational certification (54 per cent) also reported stronger co-worker support. Similarly, workers at JSCs reported higher co-worker support but again caution must be exercised due to the small number of respondents.

Employee commitment and willingness to quit

Workers are more likely to perform well and increase effort when they have a strong commitment to the organization (Walton, 1985; Porter, 1990; Womack, Jones and Roos, 1991). As discussed earlier in this chapter, commitment refers to a worker's identification and involvement in an organization and encompasses an acceptance of goals and values, working hard and a desire to stay with the organization (Porter et al., 1974: 604). High commitment has been shown to be associated with a variety of positive enterprise outcomes, such as lower turnover, lower absenteeism, higher motivation and involvement, higher job performance, a willingness to accept change and organizational citizenship behaviour (see Benson and Brown, 2007).

The perceptions discussed above underpin workers' commitment to their organization and whether they wish to continue working for the organization. Workers' general and relative health, the stress they experience on the job, their satisfaction with their work, their workloads and opportunities, and the social and supportive dynamics of the people with whom they work contribute to workers' commitment and their wish to maintain membership of the organization. In this study, 75 per cent of workers indicated a low or uncertain (unsure) level of commitment to their enterprise, which would suggest a large percentage of workers may consider quitting in the foreseeable future. This was not the case, however, with only 36 per cent of workers indicating an uncertain or high willingness to quit. This finding, in conjunction with the high levels of dissatisfaction with tasks, accountabilities, responsibilities and participation, suggest a poorly motivated and engaged workforce. As pointed out above, these results indicate the possibility of some important negative consequences for the enterprise.

As with the other issues discussed above, these critical aspects of employee perceptions varied across the various enterprise and worker demographics. Employee commitment was higher in the south (48 per cent compared to 2 per cent in the north), as was commitment among dispatched workers (55 per cent and 23 per cent, respectively). Commitment was slightly higher among older and male workers, as well as those without tertiary qualifications. Commitment was also higher for those with professional or occupational certification, which suggests commitment may be more to the profession than to the employer. Those with local *hukou* status demonstrated higher commitment, as did those with rural citizenship. Workers from SOEs and JSCs showed higher commitment although some caveats apply to the JSCs due to small numbers.

By international research standards, these levels of employee commitment are low, as are the low levels of willingness to quit. Low levels of willingness to quit was most prominent with workers from the north (88 per cent) and contract workers (64 per cent). Interestingly, a higher number of younger workers and female employees indicated low ratings for willingness to quit, as did those with tertiary qualifications, those with local *hukou* status or urban citizens. Workers in JSCs were more likely to indicate a willingness to quit, although the numbers of respondents were low. In general, workers appear to be reluctant to consider quitting as a way of overcoming some of the dissatisfaction they feel towards work. The state of the relevant labour markets may explain some of this finding, and the strong support of supervisors and co-workers may counteract some of the negative aspects of the job. Findings are presented in Table 6.5.

Conclusion

This chapter has explored the well-being and satisfaction of workers with their jobs. Most workers considered their general health to be good and nearly half felt that their health was better compared to other workers they knew of the same age. Job stress was reported as low for most workers. In general, and in contrast to the findings of Chapter 5, employees seemed to be quite dissatisfied with the main components of their jobs (tasks, account-abilities, responsibilities and participation), with over 90 per cent responding that they were dissatisfied or it was 'just alright'. Satisfaction with the job, however, may have improved slightly with just over half of the workers claiming these aspects of the job were worse five years ago.

There did not appear to be strong views that workers were suffering from work overload. Excessive workloads can be damaging to workers' health and productivity and can also restrict opportunities to take on more challenging and interesting work. This situation was not the case in this study, with many workers appearing to have routine jobs with little control and participation in decisions affecting their daily work life. This finding, coupled with the low levels of job stress, suggests a large number of disaffected workers with low motivation and productivity, workers feeling marginalized and limited opportunities for advancement.

Support from supervisors and colleagues was, however, generally high. Such support could partly explain the high levels of worker health and strong relative health. The extent of support from the people with whom workers mostly interact could also contribute to the low levels of job stress found in this study. Such support did not appear to translate to more positive perceptions by workers of the fundamentals of their jobs, in particular, the nature of tasks, accountabilities, responsibilities and participation.

Employee commitment was low, but there did not appear to be a desire to consider changing employers or jobs. This reluctance may be a result of the local labour markets in both regions, which make such considerations a little risky, or perhaps the low levels of stress and work overload compensate sufficiently for this. Yet, as discussed earlier in the chapter, high levels of commitment offer many advantages for the enterprise, including higher job performance, lower absenteeism and turnover, and a willingness to accept change. These are important outcomes, but with the Chinese economy booming at the time of the research, perhaps enterprises and managers were more concerned with labour shortages than improving productivity.

Some of the above findings can be explained using enterprise and employee characteristics. Enterprise location demonstrated some key differences which relate to the composition of industry, the type of jobs on offer and the type of employment contracts common in different regions. Enterprise ownership also led to various different perceptions, with SOEs and JSCs appearing to be different from DPEs and FIEs in some important aspects. Age and gender were important factors, but only for some of the aspects of work and well-being. Education and professional/occupational certification were important in certain aspects of the analysis but sometimes in unexpected ways. This finding may be reflecting the particular work cultures and differences compared to other industrialized economies. The possession of a local *hukou* or being an urban citizen (as opposed to a rural citizen) was also a useful explanatory factor in several aspects of work. The latter factors must, however, be understood in the wider context of domestic migrant labour.

This chapter suggests some important outcomes and lessons for the reform process. A comparison of the present findings with the results of our earlier study (Zhu, Webber and Benson, 2010) demonstrates some significant changes concerning job satisfaction. This finding would be expected given the size and significance of the restructuring process in the first two to three decades. Job stress, for example, would be expected to rise given the initial shift away from the 'iron rice bowl'. The fact that job stress remains low by comparative standards, and with job satisfaction falling further, suggests some deeper issues have arisen in the latter transition stage. Although we do not claim that the findings are representative of China as a whole, they do demonstrate some possible problems for the future and question the automatic assumptions of successful reform within a centralized control system.

As the reform process continues, enterprises will require greater focus on worker well-being and job satisfaction. Competitive, knowledge-based businesses will need a more strategic management-oriented approach to labour where HRM practices and policies are aligned with the key corporate objectives, such as productivity and economic performance. At the time of the research, workers in the enterprises involved in this study seem to be reverting to many of the previous ways of workers in State-owned enterprises (SOEs): low job satisfaction, low stress, low workloads, routine jobs with little job control, high collegial support, poor commitment and a desire to stay with the enterprise. While this finding differs from the conclusions drawn in Chapter 5, the key issues in that chapter revolved around matters that could be legislated or included in employment contracts, such as pay and the various insurances. The findings of this chapter present a different challenge for enterprises and managers: how can organizations increase employee commitment, develop more creative jobs, give a measure of control back to workers, while at the same time not diminish supervisor and co-worker support or impact on workers' health and well-being? In short, future reform will need to focus on people issues more than on structural change, which is best done at the enterprise or micro level rather than through macro-economic restructuring.

7   Future expectations among workers

Introduction

The previous chapters explored the responses by managers and workers to macro-economic restructuring and labour management reform and employees' perceptions of fairness, satisfaction and well-being at work. Enterprises of various types, in transitioning to modern contemporary organizations, were faced with a number of challenges that required a variety of management strategic initiatives with regard to skill and labour shortages, new types of workers, implementing collective agreements and approaches to resolving conflict and industrial disputes. Workers responded to these management initiatives both individually and collectively.

Overall, workers appeared to accept the macro-economic reforms, particularly those related to wages and working conditions. Perceptions of fairness, well-being and satisfaction, however, varied considerably between workers and disparities were observed by firm type, location and a number of worker characteristics. The general conclusion we reached was that future reform will need a greater focus on organizational climate and people issues rather than on structural change. This shift is unlikely to be achieved by macro-level directives but rather through enterprise or micro-level reform where workers and management jointly participate in decisions impacting on employment.

The findings reported in Chapter 6 demonstrated the challenges facing enterprises and managers in this task. High on the enterprise reform agenda will be the need to increase employee commitment, develop more creative jobs and delegate a measure of autonomy to workers. At the same time, enterprises and managers must be careful not to diminish supervisor and co-worker support or impact negatively on workers' health and well-being. This will be a difficult task as competitive businesses operating in the third decade of the twenty-first century are likely to be those that adopt a strategic management approach to labour where HRM practices and policies are aligned with the key corporate objectives such as productivity and economic performance.

This narrow focus on enterprise performance is likely to create some confusion and uncertainty for many workers and will raise questions about how confident workers are about their future employment with their present or other enterprises. Employee optimism, or a belief in the best possible outcomes in situations of uncertainty (Pearle, 1956), will be a critical component of this analysis. Optimism is not only important to give positive meaning to work (see Furnham, 1997) but also important to the development of employee commitment, work engagement and feelings of job security. Employee optimism more generally is also important in the achievement of corporate objectives as optimism has been shown to be positively related to employee performance and, in turn, organizational performance (Green, Medlin and Whitten, 2004).

This chapter will explore the level of employee optimism by analyzing major employment concerns of employees over the next five years. Exploring workers' perceptions about their future employment and drawing conclusions for policy change from these perceptions is, however, beset with difficulties. Such an analysis relies on workers' responses to what they think their future is likely to be and may vary considerably according to a range of enterprise and personal characteristics (Chan, 2005). Moreover, how workers feel today may be different to the way they felt yesterday or will feel tomorrow. We thus make the assumption that while individuals may differ, the findings, when viewed collectively, will give a reasonable representation of respondents' optimism concerning their future employment prospects.

The chapter commences with an examination of workers' optimism concerning various aspects of their current job over the next five years. This will be followed by an analysis of workers' perceptions of their employment prospects in the external labour market, in particular, whether they feel they are employable, and the pay and conditions they think they would receive. We then explore individual workers' labour market optimism over the next five years by examining how workers feel about their employment prospects compared to co-workers in similar jobs and with similar qualifications. The penultimate section considers the implications of these perceptions for macro-level policymakers and enterprise management. A short conclusion completes the chapter.

Employment in the current job over the next five years

It is difficult for workers to predict the employment environment within their present company over the next five years. At the regional or global level, conflicts, pandemics and financial crises have the ability to substantially disrupt business and commerce. This is also the case for the economic policies and legislative agendas of nations and states. At the industry or enterprise level, the quality of management, changing markets, new technology and the constant search for efficiency and productivity have demonstrated that any particular context can change rapidly and with major consequences for the internal labour market. In asking workers for their thoughts on their future employment, we are also aware that past and present experience can influence such thoughts as well as workers' current position in the labour market and their individual life experiences. Personal characteristics such as age, education and gender may also be important.

We begin this discussion by examining employees' perceptions of future job security before examining pay, work effort, working conditions and training. Each of these areas is sensitive to the macro- and enterprise-level environment. In each case, we will examine the reasons for these perceptions where the relevant data is available. We will also break down the findings, as in earlier chapters, according to a range of enterprise and worker characteristics.

Job security

The majority of workers surveyed (81 per cent) felt their jobs were secure over the next five years. As shown in Table 7.1, this percentage did not vary substantial between various groups of workers, although only 71 per cent of workers in Domestic private enterprises (DPEs) felt their jobs were secure compared to 90 per cent of workers in State-owned enterprises (SOEs). As expected, older workers, male employees, workers without tertiary qualifications or occupational certification, and those from rural areas were a little less certain of the security of their employment. Workers in the north (83 per cent) were also slightly more confident about their future than their southern counterparts (80 per cent), which may reflect the heavier concentration of tertiary industry and wealth in that region (see Table 1.1).

We asked workers the reasons for their views on the security of their jobs. The most common responses are presented in Table 7.2. In the case of workers who felt their jobs were secure, those from the north were likely to cite the employment contract, company prospects and the stability of SOEs. Whilst the first and last reason were also important to workers in the south, these workers also mentioned the difficulty of shutting down large companies and company welfare provisions. Workers who felt unsure about their jobs cited more personal reasons. Northern workers referred to their age and lack of skill, whilst workers from the south were more likely to mentioned that they were new to the job and the competitive environment within their company. Such a division is understandable given the higher percentage of women in the northern sample and the higher percentage of dispatched and professionally qualified workers in the south.

Pay

Overall, 75 per cent of workers responding to the survey felt their pay would improve over the coming five years. This was more likely to be the case for workers in enterprises located in the south (79 per cent) compared to workers in the north (71 per cent). SOE employees were the most pessimistic about wage increases, with only 66 per cent of these employees believing

Table 7.1 Employees' expectations concerning their current job over the next five years (%)

	Secure job		Increased pay		Work harder		Better conditions		Better trained	
	Yes	*No*	*Yes*	*No*	*Yes*	*No*	*Yes*	*No*	*Yes*	*No*
All workers	81	19	75	25	90	10	65	35	58	42
Enterprise location										
North	83	17	71	29	91	9	65	35	54	46
South	80	20	79	21	89	11	66	34	62	38
Worker type										
Dispatched workers	80	20	84	16	93	7	75	25	71	29
Contract workers	81	19	73	27	89	11	64	36	57	43
Age										
<35 years old	80	20	80	20	91	9	71	29	62	38
35–45	85	15	65	35	90	10	60	40	56	44
>45 years old	78	22	60	40	83	17	48	52	42	58
Gender										
Male	78	22	74	26	90	10	67	33	55	45
Female	85	15	76	24	90	10	64	36	61	39
Education										
Tertiary and above	84	16	75	25	89	11	68	32	58	42
Below tertiary	78	22	74	26	91	9	63	37	58	42
Local Hukou status										
Yes	82	18	69	31	88	12	58	42	55	45
No	80	20	83	17	92	8	74	26	62	38
Urban/rural citizen										
Urban	82	18	73	27	90	10	63	37	57	43
Rural	79	21	79	21	90	10	71	29	61	39
Certification										
Yes	83	17	77	23	91	9	72	28	62	38

(*Continued*)

Table 7.1 (Continued)

	Secure job		Increased pay		Work harder		Better conditions		Better trained	
	Yes	No	Yes	No	Yes	No	Yes	No	Yes	No
No	79	21	72	28	89	11	59	41	54	46
Enterprise ownership										
SOEs	90	10	66	34	85	15	58	42	51	49
DPEs	71	29	78	22	93	7	67	33	61	39
FIEs	84	16	79	21	92	8	67	33	60	40
JSCs	84	16	81	19	87	13	74	26	60	40

Source: Worker survey.

Table 7.2 Workers' comments regarding employment prospects in their current job

Key issues	North (Beijing and Hebei)	South (Hunan and Guangdong)
Secure job	*If Yes*: Contract constraints Company has a bright future SOE (is stable) *If No:* Older than colleagues and so will be affected Not highly skilled.	*If Yes:* SOEs (are stable) Large company, not easy to shut down Welfare is good Have signed contract with employers *If No:* Highly competitive New to the company
Better working conditions*	*If Yes:* Wages and welfare Interpersonal relationships Working hours and work intensity	*If Yes:* Wages and welfare Working environment Training and promotion
Better trained*	*If Yes:* Professional skills and knowledge Managerial skills Product knowledge Communication skills	*If Yes:* Professional skills and knowledge Managerial skills Product knowledge Safety training

Source: Worker survey.

Note: * Respondents were only asked to comment if their response was 'yes'.

their pay would rise. Significant difference also existed between various groups of workers, namely, dispatched workers, workers under 35 years of age, those without a local *hukou*, urban residents and those without professional qualifications or certification. Results are presented in Table 7.1.

Some of these findings appear to be inconsistent with workers' views concerning job security. Yet, it would be a mistake to assume that pay and job security are necessarily correlated. While we did not ask workers directly the reason for their views, it is clear that workers in SOEs valued job security (and less stressful jobs as indicated in Chapter 6) over financial rewards and that dispatched workers may consider themselves as having more freedom to negotiate market-based wages. Younger workers were also more likely to possess the skills that would be in demand in the future as were those with some professional certification. These results may also be illustrating workers' perceptions of the future of the 'dynamic' south, where market-based mechanisms are likely to lead to higher demand for the type of labour they are offering. In other words, workers who seek higher pay and other rewards cannot necessarily be classified as representative of the more generic, skill-based labour market.

Work effort

Responses received indicate that 90 per cent of employees surveyed expected to work harder in their present job over the next five years than they do at the present time. This perception was broadly confirmed by all groups of workers irrespective of location, enterprise ownership and a variety of worker characteristics. The only significant difference was that workers over 45 years of age (83 per cent), workers in SOEs (85 per cent) and, to a lesser extent, workers in Joint stock companies (JSCs) (87 per cent) were less likely to feel that way, although they still overwhelmingly felt that they would be required to make greater efforts in their work (see Table 7.1). This is a sharp increase of the assessment of current work overload discussed in Chapter 6 where only 49 per cent of workers felt they were presently overloaded with work.

Working conditions

While 75 per cent of workers felt their pay would improve over the next five years, only 65 per cent of respondents claimed this would also apply to their working conditions. This view was more likely in the case of workers in DPEs, Foreign invested enterprises (FIEs) and JSCs, which is to be expected as working conditions (but not pay) are often seen as being superior in SOEs compared to other enterprise types. Location was not an important differentiator in these perceptions, but a number of worker characteristics were significant. The most important of these characteristics were being a dispatched worker, under 35 years of age and having tertiary education qualifications and/or professional certification. Interestingly, employees without a local *hukou* or possessing rural citizenship were more confident about improvements in working conditions, suggesting a relative assessment of their previous or future employment rather than an assessment of their current employer. Results are detailed in Table 7.1.

In order to gain further understanding of these generally positive expectations concerning working conditions, we asked respondents why they felt this way. We broke down the analysis by location which seemed to be a general predictor of responses. Results are presented in Table 7.2. Workers from the north listed three major areas of work that they felt would improve: wages and welfare, interpersonal relationships, and working hours and work intensity. While workers from the south also expected wages and welfare to improve, other areas of work mentioned were matters related to the working environment, training and promotion. The expectation of improved interpersonal relationships by northern workers is understandable, as in Chapter 6 (see Table 6.5) we reported that 44 per cent of northern workers felt the level of co-worker support was low (compared to 1 per cent for workers from the south). Working hours and work intensity was somewhat surprising given that 80 per cent of northern workers assessed their level of work overload as low (see Table 6.5), although their expectations may reflect their desire to keep their present working conditions. For southern workers, the belief that the working environment will improve may reflect a more general view that in a competitive market for labour best practices will prevail. While workers from the south were more satisfied with training and promotional opportunities, the belief that these aspects of work would further improve may reflect the importance these workers, and perhaps their employers, place on these activities.

Training

Training is a critical component of work within the global economy due to the pressure of increasing competition and the shortage of skilled workforce (Benson and Zhu, 2002; Min and Zhu, 2020); it has also been a key underpinning of the macro-economic reform in China over the past four decades. Nevertheless, only 58 per cent of workers responding to our survey felt they would have better training in the coming five years. This was more likely to be the case with workers from the south (62 per cent) compared to those from the north (54 per cent) and workers from DPEs, FIEs and JSCs (61 per cent, 60 per cent and 60 per cent, respectively) compared to 51 per cent of SOE workers. Various types of workers were more likely to claim that they will be better trained in the future, including dispatched workers, workers under 35 years of age, female employees, workers with professional or occupational certification, rural citizens and those employees without a local *hukou*. Details are presented in Table 7.1.

While there were some differences in the above findings on future training when broken down by location, there was general agreement among both groups of workers as to the focus of this training (see Table 7.2). Professional skills and knowledge were seen as the critical training need which re-enforces the earlier finding that professional certification is a differentiating factor. As Chinese enterprises continue their move to high-tech manufacturing and a greater demand occurs for jobs in the tertiary sector, such training will be essential (Min and Zhu, 2020). Managerial training will be needed to accompany such a transition. As products and processes become more complex, training in product knowledge will be essential. The only notable difference in this respect between workers is that those from the north also listed improved communication skills, while those from the south emphasized safety concerns. This difference reflects, to a large extent, the nature of the industrial structure in each region and the greater job stress felt by workers in the south (see Table 6.5).

Employment prospects in the external labour market

The above analysis of employment in the internal labour market illustrated that the majority of workers in this study felt reasonably confident about their future with the company – more so about job security and wages and less so about working conditions and training. The vast majority of workers, did, however, recognize that these aspects would also entail working harder than in the past. Do these workers feel the same way about their prospects in the external labour market? In this section, we address this question by examining whether the respondents felt they are employable elsewhere, and whether they felt they would receive similar pay and working conditions in other companies.

Employability

As shown in Table 7.3, 84 per cent of workers felt they were employable elsewhere if they lost their present job. Workers from the south were more likely to feel this way than their northern counterparts (88 per cent and 79 per cent, respectively). A variety of reasons were given to support these views which, as in the previous section, we broke down by enterprise location. Workers in the north and the south felt they possessed the necessary experience and skills to gain similar work. Some workers in the north also mentioned that they had been undertaking relevant training and that this would also give them an advantage in the external labour market. Other workers in the south also pointed out that the demand for labour in that region was strong, particularly in their specific job or occupation. In contrast, workers who felt they were not employable pointed to age and, in the case of the north, to gender. Results are presented in Table 7.4. In the main, such findings reflect the dynamism of the economic zones in the south that are well oriented towards market forces.

A number of worker characteristics explained some of these differences. Contract and younger workers were clearly more confident as were male employees and those with professional or occupational certification. Workers without a local *hukou* or who had only rural citizenship were also more confident about their employment in the external labour market. While workers with a local *hukou* and urban citizenship tend to have better job security and gain the benefit of all social insurances and improved housing allowances, it may well be that these factors also constitute an obstacle to their employability elsewhere as they may be more expensive to employ. This situation is illustrated by the finding that workers in SOEs were significantly less confident than their counterparts in DPEs, FIEs and JSCs.

Pay

If workers lost their current job and needed to seek work elsewhere, would they feel they could maintain the same level of income? The majority of workers, 81 per cent of respondents, felt this would be the case; this perception was more prevalent with workers from the south than the north

Table 7.3 Employees' expectations if they lost their current job (%)

	Will be employable if lost job		Same pay if lost job		Same conditions if lost job	
	Yes	*No*	*Yes*	*No*	*Yes*	*No*
All workers	84	16	81	19	66	34
Enterprise location						
North	79	21	78	22	63	37
South	88	12	83	17	69	31
Worker type						
Dispatched workers	80	20	76	24	57	43
Contract workers	84	16	81	19	67	33
Age						
<35 years old	88	12	82	18	72	28
35–45	79	21	83	17	60	40
>45 years old	67	33	69	31	47	53
Gender						
Male	88	12	82	18	69	31
Female	78	22	80	20	62	38
Education						
Tertiary and above	85	15	81	19	69	31
Below tertiary	82	18	80	20	63	37
Local Hukou status						
Yes	77	23	78	22	61	39
No	92	8	84	16	74	26
Urban/rural citizen						
Urban	80	20	80	20	64	36
Rural	90	10	82	18	71	29
Certification						
Yes	86	14	82	18	68	32
No	81	19	80	20	65	35
Enterprise ownership						
SOEs	75	25	73	27	59	41
DPEs	87	13	82	18	67	33
FIEs	86	14	89	11	72	28
JSCs	100	0	92	8	83	17

Source: Worker survey.

(83 per cent and 78 per cent, respectively). Workers in the north felt that wages in their region for the same job and position were similar, for example, for accountants, mechanics and engineers. Respondents also mentioned that jobs were related to skill levels, which they possessed, and as their current wages were low, they believed it would be easy to get a better paying job. This latter reason contradicts to an extent the argument concerning the similarity of wages in the region. Similar reasons were, however, given by workers in the south, although respondents also mentioned the strong demand for labour. The response from southern workers is, to a large degree, an outcome of the market-oriented approach and entrepreneurship

Table 7.4 Workers' comments regarding employment prospects if they lost their current job

Key issues	North (Beijing and Hebei)	South (Hunan and Guangdong)
Employable within current labour market	*If Yes:*	*If Yes:*
	1 I am more experienced	1 I am more experienced
	2 I have skills	2 I have skills
	3 I have kept learning and making progress every day	3 Currently there are large demands for people working in my position
	If No:	*If No:*
	1 Age (is old)	1 Age (is old)
	2 Female	
Job with same pay	*If Yes:*	*If Yes:*
	1 Wage is similar for same position (e.g. accountant, mechanic, engineer)	1 For same position, wages in our company are lower than others
	2 Skill	2 Skills and experience
	3 Current wage is too low; thus, it is easy to get a better paying job	3 Large market demand
	If No:	*If No:*
	1 Age	1. Age
Job with same working conditions	*If Yes:*	*If Yes:*
	1 More experience	1 More experience
	2 More skills	2 More skills
	3 Man struggles upwards	3 Man struggles upwards
	If No:	*If No:*
	1 Hard to tell	1 Do not have much experience
	2 No idea	2 Do not know, never think about it

Source: Worker survey.

that is prevalent, as discussed earlier, in the south. Workers in the northern and southern regions who felt they would not be able to obtain a similar paying job usually identified their age as the reason (see Table 7.4).

As demonstrated in Table 7.3, some of the differences in perceptions concerning maintaining the same pay levels can be explained by four key worker demographics. Contract workers felt that they were more likely to maintain their current wages, as were workers under 45 years of age, those without a local *hukou* and those who worked in DPEs, FIEs and JSCs. Other demographic groups did not provide significant indicators in this regard. Nevertheless, it is clear that workers' perceptions about their position in the external labour market are generally optimistic both in terms of their employability and the maintenance of their current pay levels. As we shall see below, this optimism is not as strong when considering working conditions.

Working conditions

Working conditions can include not only matters relating to the way work is performed and executed and the benefits granted by the employer, but also the social climate at the workplace that can add substantially to the well-being and satisfaction of employees (Eyferth, 2006; Lee, 2007). In this context, working conditions can include aspects such as hours of work, roster arrangements, leave, work breaks, insurance, physical facilities and social relationships. Only 66 per cent of respondents felt they could maintain their present working conditions in the event of losing their job and gaining employment elsewhere. This was more likely to be the case with workers from the south (69 per cent) compared to those from the north (63 per cent). As illustrated in Table 7.4, there was agreement between workers in both locations regarding the reasons for their views, such as possession of the necessary skills and experience. There were some minor differences between regions for those who felt they would not be able to maintain their conditions, such as lack of experience of some workers in the south. Many workers found answering such a question challenging as working conditions are difficult to quantify or value until lost.

As above, we also explored possible variations in these responses due to the characteristics of this particular sample of respondents. Virtually all the demographic groups explored (see Table 7.3) were able to explain some level of variation, with the exception of the professional/occupational certification aspect. Contract workers, those under 45 years of age, male employees, those with tertiary qualifications, those without a local *hukou*, those with rural citizenship and workers in DPEs, FIEs and JSCs were more likely to feel they would gain new employment with at least the same conditions of work. However, workers tended to be less confident with regard to these conditions of work than they were regarding their future remuneration. This discrepancy partly suggests that employers may well have more flexibility in varying conditions of work than they do with regard to pay. Conditions of work may well be the silent component of rewards when workers are seeking and negotiating a new job.

Employee labour market optimism

In this section, we develop further the analysis of workers' assessments of their prospects in the internal and external labour markets over the next five years by reporting on the results to the question of whether they believed they would be better or worse off relative to others in the company with similar jobs and qualifications. This analysis includes employees' optimism concerning their current job as well as their optimism concerning their employability, future pay and working conditions if they lost that job.

Internal labour market

How then did workers feel about the security of their current job relative to other people in their company with a similar job and qualifications? Some 12 per cent of workers felt their job was more secure than similar co-workers and 5 per cent of workers felt their job was less secure. The vast majority (83 per cent) of workers felt that their job security was much the same as similar workers in their company. In comparison, 81 per cent felt their jobs were secure as reported in Table 7.1. These are, of course, responses to different questions and take into account not just their overall perceptions of worth to the enterprise but also their assessment of their performance compared to others (including other factors such as relationships with supervisors or the level of organizational commitment as discussed in the previous chapter). It is also possible that workers' optimism within the internal labour market is simply representing the wider tendency of individuals to rate themselves better than others (Ghose, 2013).

Notwithstanding, most respondents in this study felt confident about their employment over the next five years and some workers were more likely to feel this way. Workers located in the south and those employed by JSCs felt more optimistic, as did workers over 45 years of age, males and those with professional certification. A local *hukou* and/or urban citizenship did not appear to moderate these perceptions. Results are presented in Table 7.5.

Does this optimism extend to pay increases? We asked workers how their pay would change compared to other people in the company with a similar job and qualifications. Some 80 per cent of respondents felt pay would stay the same, 10 per cent believed that their pay might rise and the remaining 10 per cent felt their pay was less likely to rise than others. In other words, most employees felt pay increases relative to similar workers were unlikely over the next five years. This suggests that for the bulk of the workforce, relative pay would stay static and if pay did rise, it would be due to a more general rise in base rates. Relative changes in pay would normally occur through the performance component of the pay package, and only 20 per cent of workers collectively perceived this would affect them, and this could result in an increase or decrease in total pay.

With only 10 per cent of workers feeling optimistic about pay increases in a new job, we explored whether there was any explanation for this among various types of workers. Workers in the south, who were under 45 years of age, male, with no local *hukou* but with rural citizenship, professional

Table 7.5 Employees' optimism concerning employment improvements over the next five years (%)

	Higher job security	More pay	Similar work intensity	Better working conditions	More training	More employable	Similar pay and conditions
All workers	12	10	85	12	12	28	30
Enterprise location							
North	9	7	88	8	11	19	22
South	13	13	82	16	13	37	37
Worker type							
Dispatched workers	13	11	95	13	11	27	24
Contract workers	11	10	84	12	12	28	31
Age							
<35 years old	8	11	87	14	11	26	30
35–45	14	11	81	11	15	32	32
>45 years old	19	3	80	4	13	31	30
Gender							
Male	14	13	82	13	12	34	35
Female	8	7	89	11	13	21	24
Education							
Tertiary and above	9	9	82	12	11	26	30
Below tertiary	13	11	87	12	13	30	31
Local Hukou status							
Yes	11	7	80	9	13	27	26
No	13	14	91	15	11	30	35
Urban/rural citizen							
Urban	11	8	82	11	12	29	30
Rural	13	13	90	13	12	27	31
Certification							

(*Continued*)

Table 7.5 (Continued)

	Higher job security	More pay	Similar work intensity	Better working conditions	More training	More employable	Similar pay and conditions
Yes	13	15	85	16	15	33	35
No	10	5	84	8	9	23	26
Enterprise ownership							
SOEs	10	8	73	10	11	33	33
DPEs	12	8	89	10	8	20	24
FIEs	8	11	92	15	8	26	30
JSCs	18	19	92	51	21	49	50

Source: Worker survey.

Notes: 1. The above figure represents the percentage of workers who feel that in their present or any future job they are more likely to achieve improvements in the terms and conditions of employment compared to co-workers who have a similar job and qualifications.
2. For the question 'Will have to work harder', only a 'Yes/No' choice was given. The response for 'No' is given in the 'Same' column.

certification and those who worked for JSCs, in particular, were more confident (see Table 7.5). This figure peaked at 19 per cent for workers in JSCs; however, caution must be exercised given the small number of JSCs in the study. This finding suggests that the external labour market is not fully developed, and from our interviews we became aware that many jobs were not openly advertised and often were allocated to family and friends of key personnel in the company. The increased scrutiny which the market has placed on JSCs may have inadvertently led their workers to have a greater degree of confidence in the external labour market.

As reported and discussed earlier, 90 per cent of respondents felt that they would need to work harder over the next five years. This perception of increased work effort was not simply about increasing work intensification, although that could be part of the answer. While 85 per cent of respondents felt that they would need to work as hard as other employees in the company with a similar job and qualifications in the future, some 15 per cent of respondents felt that they would need to work harder than similar employees in the company. Such a finding is difficult to interpret, although the decline in economic growth over recent years and the marketization of work may have led more workers to be more concerned about their jobs in the future. This finding could also be related to employees' concerns about their relative health (see Table 6.2) and the increasing pressure of KPI-related performance management (as discussed in Chapters 3 and 4), although 54 per cent of workers rated their satisfaction with their present work tasks to be better than five years earlier (Table 6.4). This suggests that these perceptions do not follow a simple upward trajectory and will thus be an issue that management will need to explore thoroughly.

There were, however, some significant differences in responses when broken down by various worker characteristics. Employees in the north, dispatched workers, those under 35 years of age, females, those without tertiary qualifications, those without a local *hukou* or urban citizenship, and those who work for DPEs, FIEs and JSCs felt they would need to work harder in the future compared to other employees in their present company with similar jobs and qualifications. On this last point, the comparative figures for these enterprises were 89 per cent, 92 per cent and 92 per cent, respectively, compared with only 73 per cent for SOEs (see Table 7.5). This result provides some support for the government's recent concern about the efficiency and productivity of SOEs (Guluzade, 2020). Importantly, however, the other differences found also suggest the need for some serious consideration by the various levels of government on what appears to be increasing disparities regarding gender, access to education, employment types, and residency and citizenship status. These employee characteristics seem to have created a segmented external labour market with significantly less opportunities for some.

We also asked respondents whether their own working conditions would improve relative to others in the company with a similar job and qualifications. Most workers (82 per cent) felt working conditions would stay the same as others, although 12 per cent of respondents felt they would improve relative to other similar workers. Workers in the south were significantly more likely to feel they would have better working conditions than similar co-workers as were workers under 35 years of age, those who did not have a local *hukou*, employees with professional or occupational certification and those working in JSCs or FIEs. The results are presented in Table 7.5. As mentioned earlier, future working conditions are difficult to predict. Nevertheless, it is clear from this study that location, age, professional qualifications and certain types of enterprises can lead workers to expect superior working conditions compared to other workers undertaking similar work and with similar qualifications.

Expectations concerning training may also be an important contributor to workers' optimism as this is often the pathway to promotion, new work opportunities and supervisory roles. While 58 per cent of respondents felt they would be better trained in the next five years (see Table 7.1), only 12 per cent felt that they would receive more training than other similar co-workers. A further 8 per cent of workers felt that the training would be inferior. Workers in the south, those between the ages of 35 and 45 years, those with below tertiary qualifications, employees with a local *hukou*, professional certification and those working in JSCs, and to a lesser extent those in SOEs, were more optimistic. Although these figures are modest, it does appear that age, possessing professional or occupational qualifications and working in particular types of enterprises are important determinants in accessing relevant future training and developmental opportunities.

External labour market

If workers were to lose their current job, how would they perceive their employability, pay and conditions compared to co-workers with similar jobs and qualifications? Earlier in this chapter, we reported that 84 per cent of respondents felt they were employable in the current labour market. This figure dropped to 28 per cent of respondents claiming that they were more employable than relevant co-workers, although 64 per cent felt their employability was much the same. Only 7 per cent felt they were less employable than others. This finding does, however, represent a high level of confidence in employment prospects at the time of the survey. Workers in the south, older workers, males, those without a local *hukou*, employees with professional or occupational certification and those working in JSCs or SOEs were more likely to feel optimistic about their chances in the external labour market. The dynamic businesses in the southern economic zones, the gender division of labour more generally in China and the need for highly skilled workers appear to be key factors in these responses.

Do perceptions of employability lead to similar views concerning pay and working conditions? Some 30 per cent of respondents felt they were more likely to find jobs that paid similar pay and conditions compared to their co-workers with similar jobs and qualifications. Only 5 per cent of workers felt they were less likely to do so, with the remainder feeling they had similar chances to their co-workers. As with employability, a number of worker characteristics explained some differences in these results. Workers from the south, contract workers, males, workers with no local *hukou*, holding professional certification and working for a JSC, and to a lesser extent a SOE, were important in building the optimism of employees in the external labour market.

Implications for macro-level policymakers and enterprise management

While the findings in this chapter relate to the future expectations of workers, they are the product of macro-economic reform and the shift away from a centrally planned economy. Such reform facilitated the development of various forms of enterprise, which in turn shaped the perception of employees through enterprise management strategies and practices. Employee optimism about future positions in the labour market will thus have some important lessons and implications for government policymakers and enterprise management.

Macro-level policymakers

Much of the reform in China has been led by central government with provincial and city governments, and government agencies, including local labour bureaus, carrying out the day-to-day operational aspects of such reform. A clear line of purpose and control with these bodies and institutions is evident, representing the context in which workers expressed their future expectations. If labour markets are unable to deliver on these expectations, it is likely that employees will lose faith in the reform process and the benefits it can deliver. As discussed in Chapter 1, the central government has been concerned for some time about the growing inequality in China and the potential for widespread social disruption (IMF, 2018). Such disruption would directly challenge the goal of 'social harmony' and could lead to widespread labour unrest over issues such as wages, overtime pay, conditions of work and social insurance (see Chapter 2).

While the analysis carried out in this chapter suggests that many workers feel that their jobs are secure and they would be employable with similar pay if they lost their current job, workers also felt they would need to work harder and were less optimistic about working conditions and training. Only a small minority of workers felt that these aspects of their jobs would improve relative to other similar co-workers. About one quarter of respondents felt they we more employable than similar co-workers and close to a third would be able to receive similar pay to that earned in their present job. These findings varied significantly between worker types, various worker characteristics and enterprises. Notwithstanding whether such disparities in perceptions are of immediate concern, these do point to issues key policymakers will need to consider.

From our analysis of employee perceptions about future employment, three issues stand out as important and relevant to macro-economic policymakers. The first issue concerns the suboptimal and limited functioning of the external labour market (see also Benson and Zhu, 2002). In China, as shown in the next chapter, the concepts of internal and external labour markets do not adequately capture the nature of work and employment in present-day China. While occupational and other forms of labour market segmentation clearly exist, there are other 'hidden' aspects of labour markets that fail to be recognized and thus remain overlooked. Personal relationships, business networks, subcontracting arrangements and illegal workers should be brought within the 'economy of labour'. Second, the practice of discriminating against migrant workers, by utilizing *hukou* and citizenship status, should be reviewed. A large number of workers being paid lower wages and with limited job security not only appears to be an injustice but also leads to suboptimal organizational outcomes.

Third, enterprise location was found to be a significant determinant of employment benefits and conditions. Almost without exception, workers in the southern regions (Hunan and Guangdong) were more likely to claim that their pay and training would improve over the next five years, that they were more employable and would receive the same pay and working conditions as they do in their current employment. These workers also appeared to be more optimistic than similar co-workers with regard to job security, pay, working conditions and employable with similar pay and conditions when compared to their northern counterparts (Beijing and Hebei). While we can speculate on the reasons for this finding, our study suggests that macro policymakers need to examine the issue more deeply to ensure employee fairness and well-being are not compromised and that discriminatory practices are not allowed to prevail.

Enterprise management

Enterprises not only respond to macro-policy shifts, but also initiate and develop various forms of policies through their market-focused strategies and actions. Statutory provisions set the broad parameters to employment and work but enterprises, through the way they manage the HRM processes, can gain a competitive advantage. From our analysis of workers' perceptions of their future employment prospects, a number of issues require consideration. First, workers were not overly optimistic about their working conditions, access to training and the intensity of work. Improvement in these aspects of employment will give employees confidence that management cares and, in many cases, employees will reciprocate with improved performance. Second, most workers believed they were employable and would maintain the same level of pay in the event of losing their job. These workers were less likely to hold such optimism in relation to maintaining the same working conditions. In both cases, however, some thought needs to be given to why this might be so and what individual enterprises can do to mitigate such perceptions.

Finally, the variation in perceptions between workers from different types of enterprises, different forms of employment and different personal characteristics suggests that more work is required to ensure enterprises treat all workers equally and that they have the opportunity to develop and contribute equally to the performance of the organization. One way for the enterprise to do this is to develop a climate of optimism within the workplace where workers feel confident about their future employment, which will lead to improved individual work performance, in turn contributing to improved organizational performance (Green, Medlin and Whitten, 2004).

Conclusion

This chapter found that a number of significant differences existed among workers in their perceptions about their present employment, their position in the labour market and their overall optimism about future employment. Workers present a unique set of characteristics and a unique set of concerns, worries and optimism for their future in the labour market. This observation is well illustrated by migrant workers who often work under inferior employment terms compared to regular contract workers who feel more confident about future pay, working conditions and training. The same was often the case with workers with lower levels of education and women workers.

Many of these findings, and those throughout the book, challenge the generally held assumptions underpinning current models of labour markets (i.e. workers are generally similar, at least within occupations) that allow us to talk about a general supply and demand for labour and maintain that the market will rectify any problems that arise in the long run. We believe this study provides the impetus to develop new ways of looking at labour markets in China and elsewhere. The following chapter presents what we consider is a more appropriate and useful way to consider work and employment − an approach we call 'the economy of labour'.

8 Conceptualizing the economy of labour beyond markets

Introduction

Social scientists have generally thought about labour markets as aggregates formed by the behaviour of individuals, though more structural theories exist. Orthodox micro-economic theories exemplify the methodological individualist approach (e.g. Benjamin, Gunderson, Lemieux and Riddell, 2011), while Marxist/post-Marxist (e.g. Bellofiore and Realfonzo, 1997) and Keynesian/post-Keynesian (Harcourt, 2008) macro-economics are examples of the latter approach. Both forms of theorizing are typically deterministic – known effects follow from known causes in a predictable manner. In both forms of the theory, labour markets are regarded as institutions that exist in their own right but are affected by external social pressures – a market exists with a given set of internal laws of operation, though external forces may modify the operation of those laws.

It is the purpose of this chapter to challenge both approaches to labour markets. Using this present research and our earlier extensive work on China, we propose that the conditions of people's work are not usefully to be thought of as determined in a labour market, nor even in segmented labour markets, or indeed in any kind of market. First, we argue that Chinese workers are extremely diverse, with so many different goals and experiences that there is an indefinite variety of kinds of labour and rarely, if ever, only one instance of any kind on offer in one place at one time. Equally, Chinese enterprises have so many different kinds of demands for labour and offer so many different conditions of work and wage levels that there is an indefinite variety of jobs on offer and rarely, if ever, a single instance of each kind on offer in one place at one time. Second, we claim that labour in China is not allocated in an institution in any way separate from or even embedded in the rest of society; the allocation of labour is rather the entirety of society studied from one point of view – that of determining the conditions of people's work. Third, we observe that much of Chinese labour is not allocated in any kind of market at all, but is arranged by government fiat or through personal relationships and networks.

The chapter proposes a way in which to conceive of the allocation of labour that is sensitive to the indefinite variety, recognizes the interactions of work and society and incorporates a variety of ways of allocating labour. We call this concept the 'economy of labour' to distinguish our vision from the conceptual deficiencies associated with the term 'labour market'. We will not propose a theory of the economy of labour as such since economies of labour are societies studied from a single point of view; a 'theory of the economy of labour' does not exist separate from a theory of society. People have methodological, individualistic, institutional and class-based views about appropriate theories of society, and in each of those theories the forces driving change in economies of labour are different. What we do contend is that in each kind of theory there needs to be a concept of the economy of labour such as the one presented here. One of our tasks is, therefore, to explain how our concept can be embedded within such social theories. Furthermore, the concept has to be able to generate the principal conclusions from existing approaches to labour markets, provided that appropriate specific assumptions are added.

Although the relevance of such a concept is not limited to China, in this chapter, we will articulate these key conceptual issues by using examples from this research and our interpretation of observations through field experiences in China. We have developed these ideas based on our attempts to interpret the rich empirical data that we have obtained and accumulated over many years. In the next section, we begin by discussing standard labour market theories, which in our present classification are deterministic (microfoundational or structural). In the subsequent section, we provide the basis for the three critiques of existing accounts of labour markets which in the next section provide our conceptualization of the economy of labour. Some of the implications of this innovation, including its relations to existing conceptualizations, are detailed in the final substantive section, before the conclusion demonstrates the significance and relevance of the claims.

Setting conditions of work: labour market theories

A common understanding of a labour market is that it is an analytical construct wherein employers come together to bid for the supply of labour services offered by workers (Elliott, 1991). The concept of labour markets grew out of neoclassical economics in which it was argued that a balance between the supply and the demand for labour would be achieved by matching the sellers of labour (individual workers) with potential buyers of that labour (employers or owners of capital) at a particular price (the wage rate). Adjustments in the wage rate would ensure that the market clears. Early versions of this approach were underpinned by a number of assumptions, such as: the attractiveness of a job is measured by wage rates, all job vacancies are filled by the labour market, workers are interchangeable, the buyers and sellers of labour are perfectly informed, all jobs can be filled so that 'frictional' unemployment does not exist and an equilibrium exists between the number of buyers and sellers at a particular wage rate (see Reynolds, 1978; Boyer and Smith, 2001; Brozova, 2015).

These micro-foundational assumptions treat labour as a commodity offered for sale by potential workers who are willing to enter into contracts of employment at a particular wage rate. Orthodox theory treats the economy as being comprised of atomistic individuals (employers and employees) who interact only through exchange (Lawson 2006). Employees are rational beings who attempt to maximize the trade-off with leisure and their investments in training, while profit-maximizing employers hire labour until the extra revenue achieved by hiring labour equals the extra costs of employing that labour. The theory is closed by a market clearing assumption, in which the wage rate settled upon leads to all those wishing to work at this price to be employed and all firms seeking to hire labour at that price would be able to do so. The basics of this theory have been enriched in recent years by studies of the process of arriving at the equilibrium position (e.g. Burdett, Carillo-Tudela and Coles, 2009) and by studies of the implications of different forms of competition (e.g. Manning, 2011). In addition, an increasing variety of mathematical models have been developed to express the labour market paradigm (e.g. French and Taber, 2011) which has been applied to an increasing range of issues (e.g. Moretti, 2011). In short, there has been a relaxation of the simplistic assumptions contained in the earlier neoclassical model as outlined above.

Over this period, other labour market theorists came to recognize that a number of factors impinge on the operations of this market process (Boyer and Smith, 2001; Brozova, 2015). These factors – laws, norms and conventions that constrain or alter individual choices (Boeri and van Ours, 2008) – generalize orthodox descriptions of labour markets. Nevertheless, in defending the neoclassical model of labour markets, Reynolds (1978: 85) argued that the "warrant for these assumptions consists, not in the fact that they correspond closely to reality, but rather they yield results with considerable predictive power". Yet, this approach regards the labour market as an entity in itself, operating according to its own rules (of supply and demand), but upon which exogenous laws, norms and conventions intrude. The intrusions are regarded as being determined outside the labour market system, rather than as an intrinsic element of the labour market (Fleetwood, 2014).

A natural extension of this concept is to regard these factors (e.g. prescribed employment contracts or minimum wage legislation) as imperfections, impeding the proper operation of the labour market, rather than as social choices about what should happen in labour markets. Furthermore, the approach considers workers as divided into a few categories according to ethnicity, age, gender, residency status and the like (Lee and Wolpin, 2010). In the *China Labour Statistical Yearbook*, for example, the overall workforce is divided into categories such as age, gender, educational background, location, sector and urban versus rural status depending on household registration, namely, the *hukou* system (Zhu, Webber and Benson, 2010). These categories are pre-given and exogenous, rather than being formed by social practices, including practices within the labour market. Evidence of work histories demonstrates that people's experiences in the labour market depend heavily on chance (e.g. the characteristics of their first job) as well as on factors, such as personality and ambition, that cannot be fitted into such categories (see Wilkinson, 1981).

In addition, the existence of government intervention suggests that it is difficult to achieve equilibrium. In China, the government plays a crucial role in allocating labour through direct intervention by the local labour bureau and their controlled labour agents, or indirect influence through policy initiatives, such as job promotion forums. Meanwhile, enterprises and trade unions are also involved in the process of recruiting labour through their formal and informal networks, including their individual employees and members (Zhu, Warner and Feng, 2011).

As such, the 'invisible hand' inherent in the neoclassical model of labour markets was seen to be curtailed by the intervention of institutions such as governments, enterprises and trade unions (Brozova, 2015). This led to the rise of alternative approaches to understanding the way in which working conditions are determined, such as the approach proposed by feminists (Power, Mutari and Figart, 2003), Marxists (Portes and Walton, 1981), post-Keynesians (Area, 2014), segmented labour market theorists (Bergmann, 1974) and regulation schools (Peck, 1996). In their different ways, these perspectives integrate institutions and institutional rules into the analysis of labour markets, arguing that institutions, such as trade unions and employer groups, government bodies and industrial tribunals, and the rules governing such bodies, as well as social norms and practices (including discrimination), are critical to understanding how working conditions are determined (Whitfield, 1987; Gospel, 2011). These approaches move the study of labour markets away from the individual as the unit of analysis and towards the influence of, and interactions between, collective groups. Whereas orthodox neoclassical theorists view such institutions as market imperfections, institutional theorists regard them as legitimate players in the market, whose influence can be accommodated through collective bargaining or government-regulated industrial dispute resolution mechanisms. In this approach, conditions of work are determined at a group level, such as particular occupations or groups of workers, and are an outcome of the social and political contexts within which labour markets are embedded. The concept of power thus becomes central to the analysis of labour markets.

Whilst the neoclassical perspective reduces labour markets to the demand and supply of labour, these latter approaches accommodate social and political contexts and do not make simplistic assumptions about markets, employers and workers. These approaches also suggest that multiple markets may exist and that market imperfections are a reality of everyday industrial life and the outcome of a variety of mechanisms (Leontaridi, 1998). These segmented markets are ascribed various labels such as 'formal' and 'informal', 'organized' and 'unorganized' or 'primary' and 'secondary' (see Benson and Zhu, 2011). The formal (organized or primary) market is made up of workers in established firms who have permanent employment and receive negotiated wages and work conditions that are enforceable through various institutions. On the contrary, workers in informal (unorganized or secondary) labour markets are often "individuals, households or small groups working on their own account and as self-employed units" such as "agricultural labourers, street traders and day workers in construction" (Gospel, 2011: 14). Labour markets may also be segmented by gender, occupation, industry, ethnicity, residency status, skill, region and firm size (Hudson, 2007). Even within large firms, workers may be segmented by employment forms, such as permanent and casual employment. In addition, many employment opportunities are available only to those already in an organization (internal labour markets) or household (family labour) as opposed to being open to all workers (external labour markets). In China, a variety of worker types exists, including formal contract workers, dispatched workers, casual workers, self-employed and subcontract workers (Cooney, Biddulph and Zhu, 2013). The short-term and precarious nature of such employment forms are typified by those working as domestic servants or construction workers who work under various employment arrangements and are typically engaged by labour hire agents, subcontractors or family members.

Generally, institutional approaches maintain that "labour markets do not just emerge and usually do not find their own 'equilibrium'. They are socially and politically constructed and embedded" (Gospel, 2011: 16). That is, whilst recognizing the centrality of broader social institutions and processes, institutional approaches (like orthodox approaches) identify two entities: the labour market and the rest of society. Unlike neoclassical theorists, institutionalists regard labour markets as constructed by and embedded in social and political processes and institutions (the classic exemplar is Williamson, 1979; a more recent analysis is Ahrne, Aspers and Brunsson, 2015). Furthermore, even though institutionalists recognize a great variety of differences between firms and between individual workers, the huge differences in human experiences and expectations mean that labour market outcomes remain indeterminate; work and life experiences, a myriad of relationships and present and future expectations leave us with at best a partial and limited analysis of workers who are in full-time regular employment and who conform to an extensive range of social norms.

Neoclassical and institutional approaches to labour markets thus rest on two fundamental characteristics: first, that there exists a labour market, a sphere of activity that is in some way separable from, even if constructed by and embedded in, broader social and political processes and institutions; and second, that individuals' work experiences are in principle determined by their personal characteristics, ascribed characteristics and social institutions and norms. Both these fundamental characteristics mislead thinking about labour and employment processes and practices. While orthodox theories treat all labour as allocated within a market, in which multiple people compete to sell labour and multiple firms compete to hire labour, and either ignore other forms of allocation (e.g. labour in family businesses) or describe them 'as if' they were a market, institutional approaches query the circumstances in which markets are appropriate ways of organizing the allocation of labour.

Complexity, embedding and forms of allocating labour

The process of matching people to jobs is noisy, one in which chance/luck plays a key role (Wial, 1991). The working circumstances of individuals are determined by a large number of complexly interacting forces. Certainly, class position, gender, age and ethnicity, and other ascribed characteristics influence a person's conditions of work, and these are revealed in cross-sectional regression models (Cain, 1987). The law, enforcement agencies, employment services, unions and regional differences condition those effects (Checchi and Lucifora, 2002), but equally important are the sequences of a person's previous jobs, the accidents of corporate and regional fortunes, connections of different strength with people in different kinds of jobs, and fortunate or unfortunate encouragement or discouragement from teachers and parents (Henreksen and Dreber, 2007). For example, in China many migrant rural workers are the mainstay of the workforce in the urban industrial zones, and their industrial and urban working and living experiences enable them to establish new family businesses in their home villages when they return (Ren and Zhu, 2016). Other migrant workers, including women workers, who stay in their jobs and gain the necessary experience may be promoted into managerial positions (Xie and Zhu, 2016).

The above conditions interact in particular ways with a person's mental predisposition to take chances or be conservative, to see the potential in a situation or the risks, and to prefer change or continuity (Boudreau, Boswell, Judge and Bretz, 2001). Furthermore, the people subject to these conditions and predispositions interact with each other, not only since their choices affect what others are offered, but also since some may offer advice or provide a model for others (Montgomery, 1992). The conclusion from this recognition of complexity is that a nearly infinite variety of forms of labour exists (Farjoun and Machover, 1983); thus, life circumstances should be conceptualized as inherently stochastic rather than as deterministic in principle. A similar argument applies to the evolution of firms and the jobs they offer.

Econo-physics (the applications of the concepts of statistical physics to economics) is one attempt to provide a stochastic version of micro-foundational models, now typically identified as agent-based models

(Wright, 2005, 2008; Lux, Reitz and Samanidou, 2005; Chen and Inoue, 2013). In such models, society is regarded as being composed of entities of different types: some are people (who work and consume), some are firms (which hire labour, produce and sell) and others may be specialized investors. There are many entities in each category. Within each type of entity, individuals behave in particular ways; they can do certain things and they choose to do activities with probabilities that depend on given rules (which change as individuals learn). They can interact with each other and with individuals of other types; they work for a firm, earn wages and buy produce from other firms. Social categories, such as wages and prices, are determined according to rules, commonly market clearing rules.

This form of theorizing radically separates micro- and macro-equilibria. At any time, individuals can be in a huge variety of states, usually limited by absolute poverty (or death) and absolute riches, and for any one individual these states can be changing over time. At the same time, certain probability distributions describe the frequencies with which individuals occupy those states. Typically, for example, income distributions are shown to follow a positively skewed distribution, such as the log-normal or gamma distributions. These distributions – which are macro-states – are generally quite stable, even though at a micro-level individuals' conditions are changing. It is possible to see that important, realistic macro-conclusions are consistent with non-uniform and non-stable micro-states.

These agent-based models, however, fail to specify the relations between the processes being modelled and society at large. The social categories within the models are taken as given, as are the rules of behaviour. In this respect, agent-based models mimic the methods of orthodox theories of labour markets. Webber (2012a) provides the means for understanding the position of labour markets within society. – Lawson (2006) and Fleetwood (2011) offer a similar view – and integrating the various ways of allocating labour in China.

Webber (2012a) argues that the economy is a system of rules, formal and informal, governing and unifying the allocation of labour within and between different forms of production and different firms. This system may entail a written government plan that restricts some forms of production and delegates to others specific tasks as occurs in China. The system may comprise the assignment of quotas to firms or regions that must plan to meet targets in whatever way seems most suitable, or it may comprise more or less formal agreements between people and their employers that seek to protect both from outsiders, such as household labour. The system may even comprise more or less open searches, in which people interact principally by selling their labour at whatever price they can command from firms. In most places, all these ways of allocating labour are present in different degrees.

People are not, however, simply producers, nor is the economy the only way of organizing lives. This does not mean that the economy is one part of daily life, different from other parts that might be called politics or households. Rather, it does mean that the economy is one angle of vision into daily life – the viewpoint that focuses on the labour involved in life's daily activities (Lawson, 2006). All activities represent someone's labour, somehow organized into a more or less coherent unity, and so involve the economy. Likewise, all of life's activities are about politics, small or large scale, involving the uses of power and influence to gain ends; all are about ideology, or culture or social relationships.

Thus, all actions are at the same time economic, political, ideological, cultural and social. These aspects are not divisible. Arguments, derived from Polanyi (1944), Granovetter (1985) and later institutionalists (Streek, 2011), that the economy is embedded in social life therefore make little sense. Economy cannot conceptually be separated from social life (it is not a bit of society) and economics cannot be about one kind of action. Economics considers all actions from a single point of view and the organization of the labour involved in these actions. Equally, people do not sometimes act economically and at other times socially or politically; an action is always all of these. Therefore, people's identities are constructed from the variety of personal, group, idiosyncratic and structural conditions that underpin daily life and that are reproduced by that life.

Chaotic conditions

The ideas expressed above enable a more nuanced understanding of the conditions of people's working lives than the more deterministic approaches described in Section 2 of this chapter. Individuals should not be conceived as belonging to a particular category of workers, with each member being identical, but rather as belonging to one category (i.e. *worker*), the members of which have a wide range of characteristics that are relevant to their employment and work conditions. In addition to attributes such as education, ambition, skills and past employment conditions, there are some well-known categories that play a role in influencing people's work chances. In China, people who are relatively young (less than 35 years of age), are graduates of good universities, have urban *hukou* and have 'good parents' with a wide range of social networks have a greater probability of finding a 'good job' compared with people who do not enjoy such conditions (Ren, Zhu and Warner, 2015). The availability of people to work – whether they can work only part-time or during particular hours, for example – is another such condition. The question of what these categories are and how important they are is empirical (this is one important avenue through which empirical research informs our conceptualization). The nature of the categories and their salience differs from society to society and changes over time.

A *worker* is a person [called i], who at time [t] has a given set of characteristics, experiences and skills CV[i, t], and who offers for sale his/her labour to employers.

The CV consists of the educational record, employment history, achievements and other characteristics of the worker deemed important by society (such as gender, age, ethnicity and residency status).

Likewise, employers are not to be conceived as belonging to industries, with each member being identical, but rather as members of the one category (i.e. *employer*), the members of which are highly variable. In China, firms such as state-owned, collective-owned, private owned and foreign-invested enterprises of different size and sectors, are the dominate employers. However, there are other types of employers, including government agents, public institutions, as well as individual family business owners, social institutions and NGOs (Zhu, Webber and Benson, 2010). They all face a great variety of conditions, have different demands for technical skills and administer labour relations in a more or less bureaucratic manner. Again, the mix of the characteristics of employers changes over time and differs in different places.

An *employer*, called j, is an institution, with a given set of characteristics, experiences and goals, that engages workers of particular characteristics, experiences and skills, offering particular wages and conditions for more or less specified periods of time. 'Engagement' may be formal and contractual or informal and implicit.

Workers and employers behave in particular ways, depending on their goals and attributes. These behaviours are inherently unpredictable at an individual level, being formed from a myriad of characteristics as well as experiences; they are, in other words, described by probabilistic rules. In agent-based models, these rules need to be spelled out (again, informed by empirical research); in structural models, the rules are implicit. The actual range of behaviours in each place and time is an empirical question.

Since there is an indefinite variety of workers and another indefinite variety of employers, each overtly offering or seeking a particular mix of skills, education, wages, working conditions, experiences and attitudes and covertly offering or seeking specific gender, ethnic mix, age, disability and residential status, there is no market. Of course, an organization or other employer may be constrained by social norms to advertise for, say, a plumber, but that public advertisement is generally combined with more covert search criteria that embody experience, prejudices and other forms of statistical profiling. In general, therefore, in one place and time, there is only one or a few instances of each commodity for sale and only one or a few instances of each type of demand; commodity supply and demand imperfectly match, and may or may not be aligned through a sale or employment contract; and labour may be allocated in ways other than by a competitive search.

> An *economy of labour* comprises the social processes and institutions through which workers come to be engaged by employers, under particular conditions, to work for themselves, or to be unemployed.

Such an economy of labour may operate in a variety of ways. One example in China is small businesses that advertise job vacancies in front of the factory. Potential workers pass by and ask about the employment conditions and may obtain a job offer immediately. Other more formal processes could be the advertising of job vacancies through online sites, universities or local newspapers, followed by formal applications accompanied by a CV, a job interview and then possibly a job offer (Benson and Zhu, 2002). Introduction through family members and friends who work in a company and know there are job vacancies is also very common (Cooney et al., 2013). Hence, an economy of labour is not a special type of social institution or arrangement; it is society viewed from a particular angle – that of engaging and dismissing, of setting job conditions and wages, of producing workers and employers. In other words, all of the social phenomena that affect the processes of offering labour and of engaging labour are elements of the economy of labour – family structures, the education system, the financial system, product market conditions, the mix of formal and informal employers, as well as formal and informal regulations and processes of standardization. These are all important elements of an economy of labour. We do not conceive of an economy of labour that operates according to its own rules and is affected by external social conditions; rather those social conditions are an integral part of the economy of labour, creating the conditions of its existence and setting the terms on which jobs are sought, offered and performed.

An economy of labour also does not comprise market clearing. At a micro level, workers and employers may temporarily suspend their search for a new opportunity, but in the long run workers are eyeing better working conditions or more interesting jobs, and employers are looking for additional, more skilled, more experienced or more compliant workers. Some recent research in China focuses on new generation employees changing jobs frequently to gain improved pay and working conditions (e.g. better work-life balance and more interesting work) (Zhu and Warner, 2018). Our sample data reported in this book also demonstrate this trend, which has been discussed in earlier chapters (e.g. Chapters 3 and 4). The micro scale is in constant flux, as workers enter the economy of labour, move between employers and exit the economy of labour, as experience causes workers to adjust their wage expectations and employers their wage offers.

At a macro level, the forces of disequilibrium within the market are as strong as the forces of competition: technical change, business management strategies, changes in product market conditions, government policies and their local implementation on the one side, and ageing, changes in experience and expectations, location preferences, migration and retirement on the other side, affect the relative numbers of workers seeking jobs and employers' requirements for workers. There is always some unemployment and it generally coexists with labour shortages for some employers, for example, the high demand for skilled workers in China.

Suppose that there exists a geographical space, subdivided into jurisdictions, with geo-coded locations inside these jurisdictions. The jurisdictions might be hierarchically organized (as in neighbourhoods, towns, cities, counties, prefectures, provinces and nations). This geographical space includes workers and employers, as well as other processes and institutions that influence the behaviour of workers and employers. Some institutions (such as government job bureaus) coincide with jurisdictions at various levels in the hierarchy, but others (such as employment agencies or labour hiring firms) do not. The boundaries of jurisdictions are more or less permeable to workers and employers. As discussed in earlier chapters, in China, the government labour bureau at the provincial, city and county levels regulates and influences the behaviour of workers and employers, for example, by specifying what kind of people can be employed as regular contract workers (e.g. workers with local urban *hukou* status) or who can be engaged as dispatched or causal workers (e.g. rural migrant workers) (Cooney et al., 2013). Workers and employers thus act accordingly.

Hence, consider, to begin with, the *core process* of initiating and terminating work. This is the first level of our analysis.

- There are workers, i = 1, 2, ..., n. Worker i has a job or not, as determined by the core processes of the previous period. In period t, that job has the characteristics of a wage W[i, t] and other conditions CV[i, t] and it provides another line on the worker's experience and skill CV[i, t].
- In the period t => t + 1, the worker searches for a job. This search may be intensive and active, or it may be passive (e.g. just listening to friends or reading the newspaper). The search is conducted over a specified search area S[i, t], using methods M[i, t]. Both S and M depend on the personal characteristics of the worker and on the results of previous periods' searches.
- This worker, with CV[i, t], using M[i, t] to search in S[i, t] receives a job offer from employer j with wage W[j, t + 1]* and conditions C[j, t + 1]*, with a probability that depends on the number of employers seeking employees in that search area and using that method. The offer is then accepted or not. Then

  W[i, t + 1], C[i, t + 1] = W[i, t], C[i, t], if the job offer is not accepted,

  W[i, t + 1], C[i, t + 1] = W[j, t + 1]*, C[j, t + 1]*, if the job offer is accepted.
- From the point of view of the economy of labour, migration designates a method of search, M, and a search area, S. Likewise, seeking promotion is a search within the employing organization.

- There are employers, j = 1, 2, ... m. In period t => t + 1, employer j searches for a worker, in search area S[j, t], using methods M[j, t], offering wage W[j, t + 1]* and conditions C[j, t + 1]*. S, M, W and C depend on the employer's characteristics and on experience of past searches. The job is offered to worker i, with a probability that depends on his/her CV and on the number of workers in this search space and method. The worker to whom the job is offered may already be employed in a different job within the employer's own organization. The offer is accepted or not.

- Other workers leave employers. Some retire at a rate dependent on their age, their health, on laws and expectations about retirement, and their attachment to jobs as opposed to leisure and lower incomes. Some leave the employer to take jobs with other employers in the process described above or to return to a pre-migration residence. Finally, some are dismissed.

In this core process, institutions and processes are fixed, employers just offer jobs (or not) and fire workers (or not); workers accept the job offers (or not) and retire (or not). The principal actors in the core process are workers and employers. However, the core process is itself constituted by a set of other social processes and institutions that make the core process possible and that set the conditions under which it operates. This is the *immediate environment* of the core process, the structure within which people live their lives and employers produce. It is the second level of our analysis.

- On the part of workers, the immediate environment consists of the set of processes, institutions and regulations through which individual workers and the labour force as a whole are reproduced. These institutions, regulations and processes include the family unit, the education and health systems, credentialing systems, various forms of urban infrastructure, social expectations, regulations and norms about work and behaviour. Birth and migration rates also feature at this level. In its broadest sense, the immediate environment also includes the processes through which workers seek work (including, therefore, their dispossession from other means of making a living) with a particular set of characteristics and aptitudes.

- The immediate environment also conditions those who are seeking work and what their characteristics are. Workers here individually adjust their search space and methods or might change their attitudes towards workplace environments, pay, conditions and social status, as well as modifying the intensity of their search and the probability that they will accept a given wage-and-conditions offer. This is well demonstrated in China where, in recent years, migrant workers have been less likely to move from inland regions to coastal regions. This trend is due, at least in part, to more factories relocating from coastal into inland regions, such as the Foxconn companies which have established industrial complexes in Hunan and Sichuan provinces as assembly lines for i-phone production (China Daily, 2017).

- On the part of employers, the immediate environment consists of the set of processes, institutions and regulations through which employers are reproduced. These institutions, regulations and processes include rules about competition, factors that influence the growth of output for different products, the financial system, education and training systems for managers, the influence of unions on working conditions and the regulation of employment conditions, and state policies about taxation, trade and the like.

- One important distinction that the immediate environment produces is the mix of formal and informal work, as well as the possibilities of mobility between the two. Employers change their expectations about the wages and conditions they need to offer, as well as the search space and the methods they need to use in order to increase profitability or to change business operations in a new set of business environments. Again, this is well illustrated by the example of Foxconn where the relocation of major production lines to inland regions was based on the potential to reduce production costs, including land, construction and labour costs, as well as obtaining more preferential treatment from local governments in the inland regions (China Daily, 2017).

All of these processes and institutions in the immediate environment make possible the core process and affect the manner in which it operates. In this environment, the core actors are state agencies, unions, non-government organizations and employer organizations, as well as private corporations. These actors cause change in the number of workers, modify the CVs of the workers who enter the workforce, influence retirement rates and alter workers' expectations (that is, the probabilities that they will use this or that search method, over this or that search area, and that they will accept an offer of a particular wage and conditions). In addition, the actors cause change in the ranks of employers, including the growth or decline of existing employers, the emergence of new employers, the demand for labour of various characteristics, and preparedness to offer particular combinations of wages and conditions, thus also affecting firing behaviour.

However, the immediate environment is also subject to change. The processes, institutions and regulations through which this change occurs – the third level of analysis – are collectively denoted as the *social environment*.

- The social environment consists of the mode of operation of society as a whole, insofar as it influences the immediate environment of the core process. Broadly, this environment consists of state goals, the influences of external events and ideologies on the state and production systems, as well as the influences of employers and workers on state goals. For example, as discussed in Chapter 2 of this book, when the labour rights abuse issue became overwhelming in China, the state introduced a new Labour Contract Law to address those issues and gave more powers to the local labour arbitration authorities (Cooney et al., 2013). Together, these environmental elements caused those related systems to change, including direct changes within the systems of work conditions (e.g. minimum wages, overtime pay, rest and holiday, and social insurance).

- In addition, environmental elements influence other changes, such as changes in the training and health systems, the operation of unions, taxation and investment policies, and, more broadly, they promote change in social norms (such as around gender and work), as well as change the conditions that affect birth, death and migration rates. These elements also produce innovations in features of the immediate environment such as search methods (e.g. by creating new methods of searching for jobs or workers).

- However, the social environment is not to be understood as an external force pressing upon the immediate environment; rather it comprises the actions of people within the economy of labour and within other arenas of social life – the actions of people and of employers, conceptualized within the core process, reproduce and modify the social environment of the economy of labour.

The above discussion describes our concept of an economy of labour; it removes notions of supply and demand, eliminates ideas about equilibrium or about imperfections that prevent equilibrium and generalizes the concept of segments in the labour market. It sets economies of labour firmly within one sphere of society, understood not as a separate part of society but as one view of social processes. The *core process* of allocating labour (the interaction of employers and workers) is embedded within a set of constraints and conventions that are created in the *immediate environment* by the state and its agencies, unions, non-government organizations, employer organizations and private corporations. In turn, the immediate agents' actions are informed by state, social and political processes of the *social environment*. Employers' and workers' level of satisfaction with the outcomes of the core process influences the actions of the agents in the immediate environment, and all bear upon the deliberations and directions taken by state, social and political agents at the level of the social environment. At the same time, this concept is consistent with orthodox models (if appropriate additional assumptions are made), agent-based models of labour markets and aggregate models. We now turn to demonstrate this claim and to illustrate some implications of the conceptualization.

Demonstration and implications

Suppose that the social environment and the immediate environment are both fixed. Suppose that all employers are firms and that these firms differentiate jobs solely along the axis of the skills that they demand. Workers differ only according to skill. Knowledge about skill requirements and wage offers within firms is perfectly disseminated among potential workers. Under these conditions, the core process mimics a model of simple market competition among workers for jobs and among firms for workers. If firms have a known relationship between the number of workers of each skill that they hire and their levels of profit, their demand for labour can be calculated. If workers know the relative utility to them of leisure and work, their offers of labour can be calculated. With profit- or utility-maximizing behaviour, an equilibrium of labour supply and demand can be computed, provided that the known relationships satisfy assumptions about diminishing returns. If workers know the returns to them of investments in skill, they can invest in appropriate levels of human capital and re-calculate their offers of labour. In other words, the addition of drastic simplifying assumptions transforms the general model of the economy of labour into an orthodox labour market model.

If, by contrast, the immediate environment consists of a set of processes that produce people with different ascribed characteristics as well as different skills, and imbues those people with different expectations about life, work and wage levels, then a segmentable supply of labour exists. If employers differentiate jobs not only by wage levels and skill needs, but also by other employment conditions, such as security of tenure and prospects of promotion, and if employers know that people with different ascribed characteristics demand different wage levels and employment conditions, these employers can formulate profit-maximizing practices that segment the labour market within the boundaries of the firm, or they can decide to hire workers with only a certain kind of ascribed characteristic. Given these conditions, barriers to mobility between different categories of jobs produce segmented labour markets. Different kinds of immediate environments – the degree of legality of discrimination by race, gender, nationality, for example (Hudson, 2007) – produce different forms of segmentation.

Marxist labour market theorists begin by specifying the kind of social environment that produces a class structure, in which some people have resources (capital) and others only their capacity to work. Employers, then, are those with capital (or the firms that they own by means of that capital). Workers may be subdivided in various ways, as described by segmented labour market theorists and firms are assumed to respond by inventing discriminatory practices to take advantage of that segmentation. In addition, though, firms and their owners have an incentive to reproduce the class structure of society, so that they enjoy a monopoly over capital ownership and so that a ready supply of labour continues; this incentive may lead to forms of political action that lie outside the immediate arena of employment and work.

In other words, these three broad classes of social theory are associated with particular versions of the economy of labour that we have described.

Each requires different kinds of assumptions to simplify the general model and each specifies particular kinds of actions within the social environment, the immediate environment and the core process. We have thus proposed a general concept of the economy of labour, recognizing that the standard concepts of economies of labour are restricted by their reliance on a market metaphor. A market requires given conditions (rules of operation set by the broader immediate environment or social environment, but taken as given for the purposes of analysis) and needs the existence of suppliers and demanders of a single commodity; once this is assumed, it must also be assumed that one or only a few kinds of labour exist, and that non-market forms of allocation of labour can be ignored (or treated as if they were market allocations).

However, the economy of labour is more than just a framework from which different models of labour markets can be produced; it is also a critique of those models, pointing to the drastic simplifications that are involved in constructing them as well as to the need to recognize the great variety of different forms of formal and informal work that are performed. The economy of labour attunes us to the complexities involved in allocating workers to jobs, to the contingencies of daily life and to the interactions between the core process, the immediate environment and the social environment. In other words, the concept provides a way of understanding the significance of, and the relationships between, the varieties of ways in which orthodox or institutional accounts of the labour relation have been developed theoretically.

The economy of labour is, furthermore, a framework within which details, drawn from empirical experience of particular circumstances, can be added. In order to be consistent with the spirit of the economy of labour, these details need to be embedded in probabilistic descriptions of behaviour and must always be sensitive to the manner of interaction of the three levels of analysis. For example, it may be observed that workers tend to prefer higher as opposed to lower paying jobs and better rather than poorer working conditions (although this is not true of all workers as some people volunteer to provide medical services in war zones, for instance). Nevertheless, the social environment produces different categories of workers with different endowments of social skills and those with more social skills find it easier to find the highest paying jobs (again, this is not true for all workers as some socially skilled workers still face difficulties in finding better paid jobs). Such conditions lead to a positively skewed distribution of wages, such as the lognormal (Webber, 2012b). A social environment in which rural residents are discriminated against based on the *hukou* system in China, both in terms of access to state services and personal interactions, but where workers tend to migrate from rural areas, where jobs are more poorly paid, to urban regions where they are better paid (albeit not in the case of all workers since some migrate in the opposite direction) tends to produce an environment in which employers can discriminate against rural-urban migrants (Meng, 2014). The same situation confronts non-national residents in the USA (Hudson, 2007). In such an environment, migration may be disequilibrating.

Conclusion

This chapter has provided a new way of thinking about the way in which work is sought and offered based on the ongoing changes in China. It is a generalization of the standard ways of thinking about labour, as the previous section demonstrated, but it is also a critique of those ways for it proposes to dispense with the notion of the labour market as the central institution that governs the search for and offers of work, not only in China but globally. We reason that there are so many different kinds of people seeking work and so many different conditions of work on offer that the concept of a competitive labour market is inapplicable; that the allocation of work occurs within a set of social institutions that are, in the end, co-terminous with society as a whole; and that much labour is allocated by regulation or personal relationships rather than in some open form of transaction. These conditions render the notion of a market less useful than the alternative we have proposed. Our model is, furthermore, open to new data about the allocation of work as well as to data that specifies the particular characteristics of work in different places; it is, thus a framework within which empirical details can be added readily.

Our model can also accommodate the new forms of work and employment that have recently emerged. As some societies move to more individualistic contracts of employment, accompanying a decline in the role and power of trade unions and an increase in the prevalence of individual employment laws (Benson, 2014; Hogler, Hunt and Weiler, 2015), the economy of labour is well placed to accommodate these global changes. The economy of labour is also well placed to conceptualize recent arguments about the need to redefine labour law, away from an emphasis on the formal contract of employment and towards the performance of any type of work (Benson, 2016). Likewise, though we have not developed this argument here, our model can accommodate unpaid (e.g. domestic) and volunteer work to become an equal participant together with paid employment in the economy of labour. In comparison with existing accounts, these extensions provide a more complete understanding of the world of work and how people participate in such a world.

Many social scientists value theories or models that are reductionist in nature, which allow for simplicity and prediction. Reynolds (1978) made the point that the orthodox concept of labour markets yields results with considerable predictive power. In fact, the addition of appropriate simplifying assumptions to our concept of the economy of labour still leads to these predictions, and so our concept has not lost predictive power – it has, rather, emphasized that these predictions come at the expense of extreme simplifications. Furthermore, as the example of log-linear incomes illustrates, the economy of labour is not without its own predictive power. Finally, we argue that an understanding of the world of work in all its complexity requires a concept like the economy of labour – simplistic predictions are not the equivalent of understanding. By clarifying reality in this way, we hope to have contributed to better research and better labour and employment policies. This chapter thus provides a framework for thinking about and conducting empirical research on the ways in which labour is allocated in China and in other different kinds of societies.

9 The ongoing challenges of labour management reform in China

Introduction

Since 1979, China has implemented extensive economic and social reforms which have transformed the economy from a central planning system to a market-oriented arrangement with increasing enterprise autonomy (Zhu, Webber and Benson, 2010). Much has happened in the last decade since we conducted our previous research and published our book in 2010. In this current book, we focus on the key economic, legal and industrial policy reforms that have been implemented in the last decade and analyze how these have directly impacted on the management of labour. As depicted in Figure 1.1 in Chapter 1, the aim of this book is to address a number of key questions related to economic and market reform that directly impact on the enterprise and, in particular, on the way reform is structured and the way it manages labour. We present more detailed elaborations on our findings in the following sections and in Table 9.1 we restate the key questions and the associated major findings.

Macro-economic reform and impact on the management of labour

In Chapter 1, we posed five key research questions that needed to be addressed to understand the impact of macro-economic reform on labour over the past 10 years or so. The overall concerns of policy changes and the impact on labour management are addressed in the first question: 'What have been the key economic, legal and industrial policy reforms implemented over this time and how have they directly impacted on the management of labour?' In order to understand the general context of this study and to comprehend recent changes and impacts, Chapter 2 provides a comprehensive review on policy and regulatory initiatives for managing labour during the first three decades of economic reform and the new policy initiatives that have been implemented in the last 10 years.

In general, with respect to the changes in the last 10 years, our findings show that the various policy initiatives and accompanying regulations have

Table 9.1 Macro-economic reform, management and worker responses, and impact on employee well-being and expectations

Number	Question	Chapter	Finding
1	What have been the key economic, legal and industrial policy reforms and how have they impacted on the management of labour?	2	*New initiatives included:* • Establishing the labour contracts system. • Implementing labour dispute mediation and arbitration systems. • Expanding the social insurance system. • Introducing minimum wage standards. *Impact on the management of labour included:* • Companies were increasingly taking the initiative for the improvement of legal awareness among managers and employees. • Employees were more aware of their statutory rights and obligations. • The institutionalization of the management of labour.
2	How have management and workers responded to these reforms and influenced the management of labour and the operations of the enterprise?	3,4	*Management responses:* • Adoption of the labour contract system and 'modern management systems' with a focus on improving labour-management relations, efficiency and productivity, while at the same time increasing workers' participation, commitment and satisfaction. • Workload linked with individual performance,

(*Continued*)

Table 9.1 (Continued)

Number	Question	Chapter	Finding
			compensation and other rewards. *Workers' responses:*
			• Overall increasing pressure on performing well with higher workloads, overtime work and ongoing requirement on improving skills and qualifications based on the efficiency-driven management model.
			• Some positive changes, including increasing wages and overall income level, enhanced social insurance coverage, improvement in other benefits, and training and career development.
			• More aware of statutory rights and obligations and utilizing their voice to gain protection either within their workplace or through the external labour arbitration system.
3	What have been the specific effects on pay, conditions of work and the opportunities for promotion, training and future development?	3,4,5,6	*Major effects included:*
			• Wages and other benefits gaps getting wider.
			• The overall reward system was differentiated by enterprise ownership and location.
			• Overtime work and pay varied significantly between different types of firms.
			• The 'five social insurances and one housing

(Continued)

Number	Question	Chapter	Finding
			allowance' were applicable to most employees, but disparities and discrimination towards dispatched and non-local resident workers existed.
			• Training and career development were widely adopted, but disparity existed between workers with different positions, skills and qualifications.
			• Opportunities for promotion were available, but this was uncertain as there was no generally accepted criteria for promotion.
			• Employee participation in management did occur, but this varied by location and ownership.
4	How have the changing policies and labour management affected the well-being of employees, their level of work satisfaction, their feelings of equity and their expectations for the future?	5,6,7	*Well-being, satisfaction and optimism*:
			• Most workers considered their general health was good and nearly half felt their health was better than co-workers.
			• Job stress was reported as low for most workers, but many employees were dissatisfied with the main components of their job (tasks, accountabilities, responsibilities and participation).
			• For the majority of employees, satisfaction with the job had improved slightly with just over half

(*Continued*)

Table 9.1 (Continued)

Number	Question	Chapter	Finding
			of the workers claiming these aspects of the job were worse five years ago.
			• Many employees expressed low commitment to their current employers but did not appear to have a desire to consider changing employers (e.g. worried about being worse off or losing job).
			• Workers have generally transitioned well from the former equality-based distribution system to an equity-based system.
			• Workers who felt they were being treated unfairly engaged in a number of initiatives to hinder or resist workplace changes with the expectation of achieving a better outcome for themselves.
			• Workers were not overly optimistic about their future working conditions, access to training and the intensity of work.
			• Most workers believed they were employable and would maintain the same level of pay in the event of losing their job, but they were less likely to hold such optimism in relation to maintaining the same working conditions.
5	How can labour management and markets best be conceptualized in China and	8	*Alternative concept of labour markets:*

(*Continued*)

Number	Question	Chapter	Finding
	can such theory have application beyond China?		• Challenged conventional labour market theory and proposed an alternative model which was labelled the 'economy of labour'.

shifted from time to time in order to cope with the changes in the economic and political environment, both domestically and internationally (Chhabra and Hass, 2019). In the early years, the orientation of policy was focused more on the protection of labour rights (i.e. introducing individual and collective contracts, adopting labour dispute management mechanisms through inspection, mediation and arbitration systems, and promoting social insurances) (Cooney, Biddulph and Zhu, 2013). In more recent years, a policy shift has occurred towards a more balanced approach between ensuring business survival (i.e. easing requirements on social insurance contributions and relaxing rules on overtime work) and, at the same time, protecting workers' overall well-being. In 2020, major policy changes continued due to the onset of the COVID-19 crisis and the accompanying economic impact. In an already slowing economy, more policies aimed at saving businesses and the economy were introduced (Callick, 2020).

These findings demonstrate the ongoing effort of the various levels of government to avoid and prevent the escalation of social unrest while balancing a reasonable degree of economic growth with adequate worker protection. These objectives were to a large extent achieved by the central government by maintaining its control through a more institutionalized approach, such as establishing labour contract systems at the firm level, labour dispute mediation and arbitration systems, expanding the social insurance system and introducing minimum wage standards.

The general impact on the management of labour of these macro-economic policy reforms has been the emergence of a more institutionalized approach and a 'rule of law' orientation to labour management. Such a trajectory is demonstrated by the increasing effort made by governments at all levels (i.e. both central and local governments) to effectively implement and enforce new labour laws and regulations. In turn, companies are increasingly taking the initiative to provide training and improve legal awareness among employees. As a consequence, workers are more aware of their statutory rights and obligations; hence, they are more likely to act accordingly through open dialogue with their direct supervisor and/or the HR department and participate in employee surveys and suggestion schemes. Companies are also more aware of their legal obligations and are increasingly utilizing the law and the services of lawyers to protect their interests.

Management and workers' responses to the reforms

In order to more fully understand the firm-level responses of management and workers to the above-mentioned government initiatives, we posed the second question in Chapter 1: 'How have management and workers responded to these reforms and influenced the management of labour and the operations of the enterprise?' The findings of our research are presented in Chapters 3 and 4 which address 'management initiatives on work and labour management' and 'employees' experiences and responses to labour management reform, respectively.

Enterprise management appears to be making an increasing effort to follow the government's new initiatives by developing and implementing new management policies and practices. This trend is particularly observable in the HR domain where the labour contract system, both at an individual and the collective level, has been readily adopted. Similarly, 'modern management systems' have been implemented, including High Performance Work Systems (HPWS), or at least some of the components of such an approach, with a strong focus on improving labour management relations, efficiency and productivity, as well as increasing workers' participation, commitment and satisfaction.

The increasing diversity of the workforce, in terms of a mix of dispatched workers, migrant workers and local residential contract workers, has led to management adopting different ways of managing workers through the use of different employment contractual arrangements. Improving the firm's competitiveness, particularly through training and employee development, has also become an important enterprise strategy in many companies, and the linking of workload and individual performance with compensation and other rewards has become the norm.

For their part, workers' responses to these enterprise reforms are highlighted by the increasing pressure workers feel to perform well through increased workloads, overtime work and the ongoing necessity to improve skills and qualifications as required by the efficiency-driven management model. Workers have, however, experienced a number of positive changes which they have readily accepted, such as increasing wages and overall income levels, enhanced social insurance coverage, improvement in other benefits, and training and career development. These improvements have not, however, been spread equally between all workers. Notwithstanding, workers have also become more aware of their statutory rights and obligations and have become more vocal in requesting their rights to be protected either through enterprise-based mechanisms or through the external labour arbitration system.

Effect on pay and conditions of work

So as to explore further the effect of these macro-level reforms on employees' own individual economic and career circumstances, we posed a third question in Chapter 1: 'What have been the specific effects on pay, conditions of work and the opportunities for promotion, training and future development?' As we indicated above, wages and working conditions have improved in China; however, it is critical to understand the overall impact of labour management reforms on workers, and whether workers perceive the reforms to have led to reasonably better outcomes in their work and social life. Therefore, there are a number of chapters in this book tackling these and related issues, including Chapters 3–6.

The research results generally show that in more recent years the disparities in wages and other benefits (the wages gap) have become wider among different types of employees with different skills, qualifications, experiences and positions. The overall reward system clearly appears to be differentiated by enterprise ownership and location, where State-owned enterprises (SOEs) have adopted a more traditionally oriented pay package in comparison with privately owned firms, particularly Foreign invested enterprises (FIEs) which place more weight on employee performance. More broadly, workers in the southern regions obtain higher wages and benefits than their northern counterparts.

Working conditions, such as hours of work, have been standardized across China since the implementation of the new Labour Contract Law, which specifies a standard 8 hours per day and 40 hours per week. Notwithstanding, overtime work and pay varies significantly between different types of firms. Most companies provided the five social insurances and one housing allowance for most of their employees, but disparities clearly existed and discrimination towards dispatched and non-local resident workers is a reality.

Training and career development were also subject to wide disparities between various categories of workers. For example, ordinary frontline workers receive job orientation and basic job training, whereas employees with particular skills, such as technicians, normally receive training beyond the basic training sessions offered to ordinary workers, including position and technical skills training in order to maintain and upgrade skill levels appropriate to their jobs. Sales staff normally receive regular marketing training with up-to-date marketing information and selling skills programmes. Supervisors and managers usually receive professional management training on various issues which gives them the possibility to be promoted later to higher positions.

Opportunities for promotion were available, but this was somewhat unclear as there was no generally accepted set of criteria for promotion. What could be ascertained was that companies primarily focused on either background criteria or behaviourally oriented characteristics, but usually not both. Employee participation in management did occur, but this again varied by location and ownership. Companies located in the more southern, open economic regions (i.e. Guangdong) appeared to have adopted more employee-participation management systems in comparison with the companies located in the north and inland regions. Such practices were also more prevalent in FIEs, which is likely to be a result of the importation of international best HR practices.

Employee well-being, work satisfaction, equity and future expectations

The critical issue in understanding the impact of macro-level reforms on individual workers and society more generally is whether employees are generally better off, satisfied with their current employment conditions and jobs, perceive a fair distribution of outcomes and are optimistic about their futures. We thus posited a fourth question in Chapter 1: 'How have the changing policies and labour management affected the well-being of employees, their level of work satisfaction, their feelings of equity and their expectations for the future?' The research findings are presented in Chapters 5–7.

Our findings presented in Chapter 6 demonstrate that most workers considered their general health to be good and nearly half felt that their health was better compared to other workers they knew of the same age. Job stress was reported as low for most workers, but many employees seemed to be dissatisfied with the main components of their job (tasks, accountabilities, responsibilities and participation). For the majority of employees, satisfaction with their job has improved slightly, with just over half of the workers claiming these aspects of the job were worse five years ago. Interestingly, however, many employees expressed a low level of commitment to their current enterprise but did not appear to have any real desire to consider changing employers or jobs unless faced with the prospect of losing their current job. Whilst many factors may be at work that could explain this result, it is equally clear that the generally perceived relationship between these variables is not always a foregone conclusion.

As reported in Chapter 5, after more than four decades of market-oriented economic reform, workers have generally transitioned well from the former equality-based distribution system to an equity-based reward system. This response was not always a foregone conclusion and many workers engaged in a number of initiatives to make or resist workplace changes with the expectation of achieving a better outcome for themselves if they felt they were being treated unfairly.

Some workers were, however, clearly better off than others. This was certainly the case with the employment conditions of formal contract workers compared to dispatched workers, but did not always result in perceptions of unfairness or injustice as different historical and social backgrounds led dispatched workers to be happier with their overall income, working hours and contractual arrangements in comparison with formal contract workers. Workers with lower education and professional qualifications generally tended to be more satisfied with their jobs and to perceive working conditions as fair compared to their more highly qualified counterparts. In addition, male workers were generally more satisfied with the current pay and working conditions than female workers who face the daily difficulty of balancing work and family responsibilities. Younger generation employees (under 35 years) were less satisfied with their current income and working conditions compared to older employees (35 years and older). The overall level of satisfaction among the workers with local *hukou*, particularly those with an urban *hukou*, is much higher than among migrant workers with rural *hukou* status. Given the unequal treatment between these groups of workers, such as the payment of the five insurances, the rural and urban divide clearly remains an issue in the labour market.

Employees generally have some perceptions about their future and their level of employment optimism. Such perceptions are important for workers as they drive motivation, enterprise commitment and willingness to undergo training and development. These issues are discussed in Chapter 7, which explores workers' future expectations and discusses the implications of these perceptions for macro-level policy makers and enterprise management. In general, workers were not overly optimistic about their future working conditions, access to training and the intensity of work. Whilst most workers believed they were employable and would maintain the same level of pay in the event of losing their job, they were less likely to hold such optimism in relationship to maintaining the same working conditions. This finding has important implications for management as often it is the non-pay related elements of the reward system that encourages workers to remain in their current job or seek employment elsewhere.

Conceptualization of labour management and markets in China

In Chapter 1, we discussed the possibility of considering new ways of thinking about the way in which work is sought and offered based on the ongoing changes in China. Thus, the fifth question posed in Chapter 1 was 'How can labour management and markets best be conceptualized in China and can such theory have application beyond China?' This is an important question to ask and the outcomes of our deliberations on this matter are presented in Chapter 8.

Chapter 8 provides a theoretical discussion on this question which utilizes the experiences and findings of our fieldwork for this project and our collective findings of our many years of research on China. We challenge conventional, deterministic theories and approaches to labour markets based on the ongoing changes in China which lead to an alternative concept that we have termed the 'economy of labour'. This argument progresses by discussing the deficiencies of conventional labour market approaches and proposing a new way of thinking about the ways in which work is sought and offered.

The concept of the economy of labour is well placed to accommodate the global changes currently taking place as well as to conceptualize recent arguments about the need to redefine labour law, away from an emphasis on the formal contract of employment and towards the performance of any type of work by any type of labour (Benson, 2016). In addition, our model also accommodates unpaid (e.g. domestic) and volunteer workers as equal participants alongside regular employees in the economy of labour. In comparison with existing accounts, this conceptualization provides a more complete understanding of the real world of work and how people participate in this world.

Conclusion

In the last decade, China has experienced immense economic and societal changes. Both international tensions (e.g. the trade dispute between China and the US) and ongoing domestic economic slowdown and social instability (e.g. labour unrest) have created pressures for further reforms of economic policy in general, and labour management policy in particular. Such reforms are driven by the need to maintain social stability (i.e. *weiwen*), improve overall economic and firm level efficiency and competitiveness, and ensure greater labour market flexibility. These elements have become the dominant agenda for the central and local governments as well as for management at the firm level. This book provides an analysis of the impact of the policy reform through a detailed examination of different types of firms with different ownership structures and in different locations with a focus on management initiatives and workers' responses. In this chapter, we have summarized our findings related to the five research questions posed in Chapter 1, concerning past and present policy developments, changing structure and strategy, new management practices and the interaction between management and workers.

Overall, the research presents a diverse picture of the current labour management situation in China. We have compared and contrasted the key elements of government policy and regulations as well as structural reform of the system governing labour management between the earlier 30 years of economic reform and the more recent 10 years of changes. We have also identified the trends and patterns of the new management systems and practices, and the impact on workers. By using both management and workers' responses, we present a comprehensive analysis regarding the overall situation of labour management, not only at the macro level, but also at meso and micro levels.

There are a number of theoretical and practical implications arising from the research. The major theoretical contribution is a new conceptualization of the way work is sought and offered in China, which was presented in Chapter 8. We contend that the concept of the economy of labour will be more useful in understanding labour management in China (and elsewhere) than traditional labour market theory and has the added ability to readily incorporate social changes and to be inclusive of all those who participate in the world of work. The research also contributes to our understanding of how governments balance the dual objectives of progressing societal transformation (i.e. better economic development, education, income and overall well-being) and improving the institutionalized environment for labour management. The research findings provide some key pointers for the future development of an economy towards a more 'rule of law' oriented society in developing nations.

A third key theoretical implication is that the research provides a new understanding of single party ruled societies, such as China, and whether the governing system is based on an ideology-driven or pragmatic-driven approach. Under the CCP leadership, China has been seen by many as a 'communist society' with a single party and ideological control. Whilst this may be the case to a significant extent, an analysis such as undertaken in this research suggests that the reality of governing Chinese society could be different. Clearly, many 'socialist' and 'communist' ideals exist in the government's propaganda and political approach. Nevertheless, as the findings presented in this book show, governments at various levels have attempted, through various policy choices, to maintain a balance between promoting economic growth and protecting workers' rights and interests.

For policymakers at both government and firm levels, the research findings have a number of practical implications. As we discussed earlier, there is an increasing need for managing different types of workers with different policy approaches. The needs of older and younger workers are very different, and the levels of satisfaction among dispatched workers, migrant workers and local residential contract workers vary depending on enterprise and employee characteristics. As the reform process continues, governments and firms will need to focus more on workers' well-being and satisfaction with their jobs and career development. Management will need to adopt a more strategic approach to labour and align practices with the key economic and financial corporate objectives. Equally, however, enterprise-level workers will need to be involved in corporate decision-making and be provided with the means to communicate openly with management. Corporate performance goals and firm-level competitiveness rely on increasing employee commitment, providing more creative jobs, allowing workers more control over their daily work life, while at the same time ensuring supervisor and co-worker support is maintained. Positive outcomes in workers' health and well-being will be a critical element in this success. In short, future reform will need to focus on people issues as well as structural change. This is best done at the enterprise or micro level rather than through macro-economic restructuring.

There is, however, a need for future research to explore these issues further and to investigate a number of challenging issues for the future development of China's labour management system (Park, 2016). These issues include:

1   The most effective way to enforce new labour laws.
2   The function of social insurances, particularly for the older generation of employees given they are facing retirement soon.
3   Adopting more empowerment-oriented HR management practices, particularly for the younger generation of employees.
4   Lowering the institutional barriers to labour mobility.
5   Correcting skill mismatches in the economy of labour.
6   Sustaining growth through innovation, and industrial and service upgrading.

The latter is especially important as rising wages continue to squeeze China's competitiveness and further global competitiveness will be based on new skills and innovation (Min and Zhu, 2020).

There are, of course, many other issues that could be developed as future research themes, and we list in this chapter the above areas based on our observations and findings presented in this book. Importantly, a key outcome of this analysis is that there is no single model that can fully explain how to develop a labour management system effectively. The different examples identify some similar but also different characteristics due to the different trajectories of history (the planning economy which saw the emergence of SOEs versus the market economy where DPEs, FIEs and JSCs emerged) and the economic, social, political and cultural contexts of the society and the firm. This heterogeneity once again establishes the importance of contextual contingencies at various levels (e.g. macro, meso and micro), and different times and locations. This complexity is further exacerbated by the expansion of Western-derived 'best practices' and management philosophies (e.g. High Performance Work Systems and Modern Management Systems), which often encounter challenges from indigenous ways of thinking and acting, making partial adoption and continuous modification the norm.

Finally, we hope by presenting in this book our research findings and suggestions for future research, we can contribute to greater dialogue and debate on China's social and economic transformation in general, and labour management and the economy of labour in particular. If this possibility is even partially realized, it may lead to some important lessons for other developing economies, and their enterprises and workers.

Bibliography

Ahrne, G., Aspers, P., Brunsson, N., 2015. The organization of markets. *Organ. Stud. 36*, 7–27.

Area, N.T., 2014. The demand for labour: a post Keynesian appraisal. *Iber. J. History Economic Thought 1*, 38–50.

Author's interviews, 2019 Interviews conducted by Ying Zhu in Guangdong and Fujian provinces in May, 2019.

Bellofiore, R., Realfonzo, R., 1997. Finance and the labour theory of value: Toward a macroeconomic theory of distribution from a monetary perspective. *Int. J. Political Economy 27*, 97–118.

Benjamin, D., Gunderson, M., Lemieux, T., Riddell, C., 2011. *Labour Market Economics* (7th ed), McGraw-Hill Ryerson, Toronto Canada.

Benson, J., 2014. Conflict resolution in Japan. In: Roche, W.K., Teague, P., Colvin, A.J.S. (eds.), *The Oxford Handbook of Conflict Management in Organisations*. Oxford University Press, Oxford UK. pp. 385–404.

Benson, J., 2016. Labour market regulation in Asia: The growing dominance of market-based mechanisms. In: Brodie, D., Busby, N., Zahn, N. (eds.), *The Future Regulation of Work*. Palgrave McMillan, London. pp. 107–124.

Benson, J., Brown, M., 2007. Knowledge workers: What keeps them committed; what turns them away. *Work, Employ. Soc. 21*(1), 121–141.

Benson, J., Zhu, Y., 1999. Market, firms and workers in Chinese state-owned enterprises. *Hum. Resour. Manag. J. 9*(4), 58–74.

Benson, J., Zhu, Y., 2002. The emerging external labor market and the impact on enterprise's human resource development in China. *Hum. Resour. Dev. Q. 13*(4), 449–466.

Benson, J., Zhu, Y. (eds.), 2011. *The Dynamics of Asian Labour Markets: Balancing Control and Flexibility*. Routledge, London and New York.

Benson, J., Debroux, P., Yuasa, M., 1998. Labour management in Chinese-based enterprises: The challenge of flexibility. *Bus. Contemporary World 10*(4), 633–661.

Benson, J., Debroux, P., Yuasa, M., Zhu, Y., 2000. Flexibility and labour management: Chinese manufacturing enterprises in the 1990s. *Int. J. Hum. Resour. Manag. 11*(2), 183–196.

Bergmann, B.R., 1974. Occupational segregation, wages and profits when employers discriminate by race or sex. *East. Economic J. 1*, 103–110.

Bierhoff, H.W., Cohen, R.L., Greenberg, J. (eds.), 1986. *Justice in Social Relations*. Plenum Press, New York.

Bies, R.J., 2001. Interactional (in)justice: The sacred and the profane. In: Greenberg, J., Cropanzano, R. (eds.), *Advances in Organizational Justice*. Stanford University Press, Stanford, CA. pp. 89–118.

Bies, R.J., Tripp, T.M., 1996. Beyond distrust: "Getting even" and the need for revenge. In: Kramer, R.M., Tyler, T.R. (eds.), *Trust in Organizations: Frontiers of Theory and Research*. Sage, London. pp. 246–260.

Blejer, M., 1991. *China: Economic Reform and Macroeconomic Management*. International Monetary Fund, Washington, D.C.

Boeri, T., van Ours, J., 2008. *The Economics of Imperfect Labour Markets*. Princeton University Press, Princeton NJ.

Boudreau, J.W., Boswell, W.R., Judge, T.A., Bretz, R.D., 2001. Personality and cognitive ability as predictors of job search among employed managers. *Pers. Psychol. 54*, 25–50.

Boxall, P., Purcell, J., 2003. *Strategy and Human Resource Management*. Palgrave Mcmillan, Basingstoke and New York.

Boyer, G., Smith, R., 2001. The development of the neoclassical tradition in labour economics. *Ind. Labour Relat. Rev. 54*(2), 199–223.

Brozova, D., 2015. Modern labour economics: The neoclassical paradigm with institutional context. *Precedia Economics Financ. 30*, 50–56.

BSY, 2018. *Beijing Statistical Yearbook 2018*. China Statistics Press, Beijing.

Burdett, K., Carillo-Tudela, C., Coles, M., 2009. *Human capital accumulation and labour market equilibrium*, EZA Discussion Paper No. 4215.

Cain, G.G., 1987. The economic analysis of labour market discrimination: A survey. In: Ashenfelter, O.C., Layard, R. (eds.), *Handbook of Labor Economics Vol 1*. Elsevier, Amsterdam. pp. 693–785.

Callick, R., 5 May, 2020. '*The prospects for China's post–Covid-19 economy*'. The Lowy Institute, https://www.lowyinstitute.org/the-interpreter/prospects-china-s-post-covid-19-economy [accessed 26 May 2020].

Chan, A., 2005. Recent trends in Chinese labour issues – Signs of change. *China Perspect. 57*, 1–13.

Checchi, D., Lucifora, C., 2002. Unions and labour market institutions in Europe. *Economic Policy 17*, 361–408.

Chen, C.-F., 2011. The antecedents and consequences of job stress of flight attendants – Evidence from Taiwan. *J. Air Transp. Manag. 17*(4), 253–255.

Chen, H., Inoue, J., 2013. Statistical mechanics of labour markets. In: Abergel, F., Chakrabati, B.K., Chakraborti, A., Ghosh, A. (eds.), *Econophysics of Systemic Risk and Network Dynamics*. Springer-Verlag Italia, Milan. pp. 157–171.

Chhabra, T., Hass, R., September 2019. '*Global China: Domestic politics and foreign policy*'. Brookings. https://www.brookings.edu/research/global-china-domestic-politics-and-foreign-policy/ [accessed 26 May 2020].

China Briefing, 12 September 2019a. China's social security system: An explainer, *China Briefing*, published by. Dezan Shira & Association, https://www.china-briefing.com/news/chinas-social-security-system-explainer/ [accessed 2 January 2020].

China Briefing, 28 March 2019b. China cuts social insurance costs for employers, *China Briefing*, published by. Dezan Shira & Association, https://www.china-briefing.com/news/china-cuts-social-insurance-costs-employers/ [accessed 2 February 2020].

China Daily, 2017. Foxconn ramps up Hunan plant, *China Daily*, 2 May, http://www.chinadaily.com.cn/business/2017-05/02/content_29158931.htm [accessed 1 May 2018].

Cohen, R.L., 1987. Distributive justice: Theory and research. *Soc. Justice Res.* *1*(1), 19–40.

Collins, B.J., Mossholder, K.W., 2014. Fairness means more to some than others: Interactional fairness, job embeddedness, and discretionary work behaviors. *J. Manag. 43*(2), 293–318.

Cooney, S., Biddulph, S., Zhu, Y., 2013. *Law and Fair Work in China.* Routledge, London and New York.

Coopey, J., Hartley, J., 1991. Reconsidering the case of organizational commitment. *Hum. Resour. Manag. J. 1*(3), 18–32.

Cronbach, L.J., 1951. Coefficient alpha and the internal structure of tests. *Psychometrika 16*, 297–334.

Deutsch, M., 1985. *Distributive Justice: A Social-Psychological Perspective.* Yale University Press, New Haven.

Elliott, R., 1991. *Labour Economics: A Comparative Text.* McGraw-Hill, London.

Eyferth, J. (ed.), 2006. *How China Works: Perspectives on the Twentieth-Century Industrial Workplace.* Routledge, London and New York.

Farjoun, E., Machover, M., 1983. *Laws of Chaos: A Probabilistic Approach to Political Economy.* Verso, London.

Feng, L., 2017. Building employee-centered work patterns of trade unions. In: Tang, T.F. (ed.), *Annual Report on Shenzhen's Labor Relationship (2017).* Social Science Academic Press, Beijing. pp. 157–167.

Flannery, R. 2020. Factories facing "severe" labor shortages in China, U.S. business group says, *Forbes,* 17 February, https://www.forbes.com/sites/russellflannery/2020/02/17/factories-facing-severe-labor-shortages-in-china-u-s-business-group-says/#566eb0736299 [accessed 28 April 2020].

Fleetwood, S., 2011. Sketching a socio-economic model of labour markets. *Camb. J. Econ. 35*, 15–38.

Fleetwood, S. 2014. From labour market institutions to an alternative model of labour markets, *Forum for Social Economics,* http://dx.doi.org/10.1080/07360932. 2014.970567 [accessed 10 November 2015].

Folger, R., Greenberg, J., 1985. Procedural justice: An interpretive analysis of personnel systems. In: Rowland, K., Ferris, G. (eds.), *Research in Personnel and Human Resources Management Vol. 3.* JAI Press, Greenwich, CT. pp. 141–183.

French, E., Taber, C., 2011. Identification of models of the labor market. In: Ashenfelter, O., Card, D. (eds.), *Handbook of Labor Economics* (Vol. 4, Part A). Elsevier, Amsterdam. pp. 537–617.

Frese, M., Kring, W., Soose, A., Zempel, J., 1996. Personal initiative at work: Differences between East and West Germany. *Acad. Manag. J. 39*(1), 37–64.

Furnham, A., 1997. The half full or half empty glass: The views of the economic optimist vs pessimist. *Hum. Relat. 50*(2), 197–209.

Ghose, T. 2013. Everyone thinks they are above average, *CBS,* 7 February, https://www.cbsnews.com/news/everyone-thinks-they-are-above-average/ [accessed 23 May 2020].

Gospel, H., 2011. Labour markets in theory and practice: perspectives from Western industrial countries. In: Benson, J., Zhu, Y. (eds.), *The Dynamics of Asian Labour Markets: Balancing Control and Flexibility.* Routledge, London and New York. pp. 11–32.

Granovetter, M., 1985. Economic action and social structure: The problem of embeddedness. *Am. J. Sociol. 91*, 481–510.

Green, K.W., Medlin, B., Whitten, D., 2004. Developing optimism to improve performance: An approach for the manufacturing sector. *Ind. Manag. Data Syst.* *104*(2), 106–114.

Greenberg, J., Ashton-James, C.E., Ashkanasy, N.M., 2007. Social comparison processes in organizations. *Organ. Behav. Hum. Decis. Process. 102*, 22–41.

Guluzade, A. 2020. How reform has made China's state-owned enterprises stronger, *World Economic Forum*, 21 May, https://www.weforum.org/agenda/2020/05/how-reform-has-made-chinas-state-owned-enterprises-stronger/ [accessed 7 June 2020].

Harcourt, G.C., 2008. *The Structure of Post-Keynesian Economics*. Cambridge University Press, Cambridge UK.

Harshana, P., 2018. Work related stress: A literature review. *Ann. Soc. Sci. Manag. Stud. 2*(3), 59–65.

Henreksen, M. and Dreber, A. 2007. Female career success: Institutions, path dependence and psychology, *Social Science Research Network*, http://ssrn.com/abstract=996873 [accessed 11 December 2015].

Hesse-Biber, S.N., Leavy, P., 2011. *The Practice of Social Research* (2nd ed). Sage, Los Angeles.

Hogler, R.L., Hunt, H.G., Weiler, S., 2015. Killing unions with culture: Institutions, inequality and the effects of labor's decline in the United States. *Empl. Responsibilities Rights J. 27*, 63–79.

House, J., 1981. *Work Stress and Social Support*. Addison-Wesley, Reading, MA.

Hsu, R., 1991. *Economic Theories in China 1979-1988*. Cambridge University Press, Cambridge.

Hudson, K., 2007. The new labor market segmentation: Labor market dualism in the new economy. *Soc. Sci. Res. 36*, 286–312.

ICLG. 30 March, 2020. *China: Employment and Labour Law 2020*. ICLG.com, https://iclg.com/practice-areas/employment-and-labour-laws-and-regulations/china [accessed 10 May 2020].

IMF 2018. *Inequality in China – Trends, drivers and policy remedies*, IMF Working Paper, WP/18/127, June.

Iverson, R., 1992. '*Employee Intent to Stay: An Empirical Test of a Revision of the Price and Mueller Model*', Unpublished Doctoral Dissertation. University of Iowa.

Iverson, R., 1996. Employee acceptance of organizational change: The role of organizational commitment. *Int. J. Hum. Resour. Management*, *7*(1), 122–149.

Jiang, C. 2018. Most employees in China looking to switch jobs, survey finds, *China Daily*, 28 March, https://www.chinadaily.com.cn/a/201803/28/WS5abb68aba3105cdcf6514e2f.html [accessed 9 December 2019].

Jung, H.S., Yoon, H.H., 2014. Antecedents and consequences of employees' job stress in a foodservice industry: Focused on emotional labour and turnover intent. *Int. J. Hospitality Manag. 38* (April), 84–88.

Kleinberg, R., 1990. *China's 'Opening' to the Outside World: The Experiment with Foreign Capitalism*. Westview Press, Boulder.

Konovsky, M.A., 2000. Understanding procedural justice and its impact on business organizations. *J. Manag. 26*(3), 489–511.

Konovsky, M.A., Cropanzano, R., 1991. Perceived fairness of employee drug testing as a predictor of employee attitudes and job performance. *J. Appl. Psychol. 76*, 698–707.

Korsgaard, M.A., Meglino, B.M., Lester, S.W., Jeong, S.S., 2010. Paying you back or paying me forward: Understanding rewarded and unrewarded organizational citizenship behavior. *J. Appl. Psychol. 95*(2), 277–290.

Lardy, N., 1994. *China in the World Economy.* Institute for International Economics, Washington D.C.

Lawson, T., 2006. The nature of heterodox economics. *Camb. J. Econ. 30*, 483–505.

Lee, C.K. (ed.), 2007. *Working in China: Ethnographies of Labor and Workplace Transformation.* Routledge, London and New York.

Lee, D., Wolpin, K.I., 2010. Accounting for wage and employment changes in the US from 1968–2000: A dynamic model of labour market equilibrium. *J. Econom. 156*, 68–85.

Lee, J., Jensen, J.M., 2014. The effects of active constructive and passive corrective leadership on workplace incivility and the mediating role of fairness perceptions. *Group. Organ. Manag. 39*(4), 416–443.

Leontaridi, M.R., 1998. Segmented labour markets: theory and evidence. *J. Economic Surv. 12*, 63–101.

Leventhal, G.S., Karuza, J., Fry, W.R., 1980. Beyond fairness: A theory of allocation preferences. In: Mikula, G. (ed.), *Justice and Social Interaction.* Springer-Verlag, New York. pp. 167–218.

Li, J., 1991. *Taxation in the PR China.* Praeger, New York.

Lind, E.A., 2001. Fairness heuristic theory: Justice judgments as pivotal cognitions in organizational relations. In: Greenberg, J., Cropanzano, R. (eds.), *Advances in Organizational Relations.* Stanford University Press, Stanford, CA. pp. 56–88.

Lind, E.A., Tyler, T.R., 1988. *The Social Psychology of Procedural Justice.* Plenum Press, New York.

Liu, J., Chen, M.M., 2017. Cohesion plan: Construction of enterprise communication mechanism for resolving labor disputes. In: Tang, T.F. (ed.), *Annual Report on Shenzhen's Labor Relationship (2017).* Social Science Academic Press, Beijing. pp. 185–193.

Lux, T., Reitz, S., Samanidou, E. (eds.), 2005. *Nonlinear Dynamics and Heterogeneous Agents.* Springer, Berlin.

Manning, A., 2011. Imperfect competition in the labour market. In: Ashenfelter, O., Card, D., *The Handbook of Labour Economics.* Elsevier, Amsterdam. pp. 973–1041.

Meng, X., 2014. Rural-urban migration in China. In: Fan, S.G., Kanbur, R., Wei, S.J., Zhang, X.B. (eds.), *The Oxford Companion to the Economics of China.* Oxford University Press, Oxford UK. pp. 382–387.

Meyer, J., Allen, N., 1997. *Commitment in the Workplace: Theory, Research, and Application.* Sage, Thousand Oaks, California.

Michaels, C., Spector, P., 1982. Causes of employee turnover: A test of the Mobley, Griffeth, Hand and Meglino model. *J. Appl. Psychol. 67*, 53–59.

Miles, M.B., Huberman, A.M., Saldana, J., 2014. *Qualitative Data Analysis* (3rd ed). Sage, Thousand Oaks, California.

Min, M., Zhu, Y., 2020. *Improving Competitiveness through Human Resource Development in China: The Role of Vocational Education.* Routledge, London and New York.

Min, M., Bambacas, M., Zhu, Y., 2017. *Strategic Human Resource Management in China: A Multiple Perspective.* Routledge, London and New York.

Min, M., Zhu, Y., Bambacas, M., 2018. Implementing HPWS among the indigenous companies in China: Analysis from both managers' and employees' perspectives. *J. Gen. Manag. 43*(4), 175–187.

Min, M., Zhu, Y., Bambacas, M., 2020. The mediating effect of trust on the relationship between high performance work systems and employee outcomes among Chinese indigenous firms. *Asia Pac. J. Hum. Resour., 58*, 399–426.

Montgomery, J.D., 1992. Job search and network composition: Implications of the strength-of-weak-ties hypothesis. *Am. Sociological Rev. 57*, 586–596.

Moretti, E., 2011. Local labor markets. In Ashenfelter, O., Card, D. (eds.), *Handbook of Labor Economics*, Vol. 4, Part B. Elsevier, Amsterdam The Netherlands. pp. 1237–1313.

Mowday, R., Porter, L., Steers, R., 1982. *Employee-Organization Linkages: The Psychology of Commitment, Absenteeism and Turnover.* Academic Press, New York.

Mowday, R., Steers, R., Porter, L., 1979. The measurement of organizational commitment. *J. Vocational Behav. 14*(2), 224–247.

NBS (National Bureau of Statistics of China), 2017. Gini coefficient in China: Inequality of income distribution in China from 2005 to 2016, https://www. statista.com/statistics/250400/inequality-of-income-distribution-in-china-based-on-the-gini-index/ [accessed 23 November 2017].

NBS (National Bureau of Statistics of China), 2019. *National Data 2019.* China Statistics Press, Beijing. http://data.stats.gov.cn/english/easyquery.htm?cn=E0103& f=912 [accessed 6 November 2019].

Ni, Z.C., 2017. A study on labor supply in Shenzhen in 2016. In: Tang, T.F. (ed.), *Annual Report on Shenzhen's Labor Relationship (2017).* Social Science Academic Press, Beijing. pp. 39–49.

Nightingale, D., Wander, S., 2011. *Informal and nonstandard employment in the United States, The Urban Brief 20*, August: 1–7. The Urban Institute, Washington DC. the United States.

Park, A. 2016. 'Rising wages, labour regulation, and the future of employment in China, *Global Network Perspectives*, 5 January, https://globalnetwork.io/ perspectives/2016/01/rising-wages-labour-regulation-and-future-employment-china [accessed 22 June 2020].

Pearle, N.V., 1956. *The Power of Positive Thinking.* Prentice-Hall, Englewood Cliffs, NJ.

Peck, J., 1996. *Work-Place: The Social Regulation of Labor Markets.* Guilford, New York.

Polanyi, K., 1944. *The Great Transformation.* Farrer and Rinehart, New York.

Porter, L., Steers, R., Mowday, R., Boulian, P., 1974. Organizational commitment, job satisfaction, and turnover amongst psychiatric technicians. *J. Appl. Psychol. 59*(5), 603–609.

Porter, M., 1990. *The Competitive Advantage of Nations.* MacMillan, London.

Portes, A., Walton, J., 1981. *Labor, Class and the International System.* Academic Press, New York.

Power, M., Mutari, E., Figart, D.M., 2003. Beyond markets: Wage setting and the methodology of feminist political economy. In: Kuiper, E., Barket, D.K. (eds.), *Towards a Feminist Philosophy of Economics.* Routledge, London. pp. 70–86.

Price, J., 1997. Handbook of organizational measurement. *Int. J. Manpow. 18*(4–6), 305–558.

Price, J., Mueller, C., 1981. *Professional Turnover: The Case of Nurses.* SP Medical and Scientific, New York.

Ren, S., Zhu, Y., 2016. Developing family businesses through ongoing learning: Case studies of Chinese urban and rural family businesses under market-oriented reforms. *J. Gen. Manag. 41*(4), 51–70.

Ren, S., Xie, Y., Zhu, Y., Warner, W., 2018. New generation employees' preferences towards leadership style in China. *Asia Pac. Bus. Rev. 24*(4), 437–458.

Ren, S., Zhu, Y., Warner, M., 2015. Dilemmas concerning the employment of university graduates in China. *Stud. High. Educ. 42*(3), 551–571.

Research Group, 2018. Research on new employment forms under the internet economy. In: Tang, T.F. (ed.), *Annual Report on Shenzhen's Labor Relationship (2018)*. Social Science Academic Press, Beijing. pp. 21–31.

Reynolds, L., 1978. *Labor Economics and Labor Relations*. Prentice-Hall, Englewood Cliffs, NJ.

Riskin, C., 1988. *China's Political Economy: The Quest for Development Since 1949*. Oxford University Press, Oxford.

Sardana, D., Zhu, Y., 2017. *Conducting Business in China and India: A Comparative and Contextual Analysis*. Palgrave Macmillan, London and New York.

Sheahan, J., 1986. *Alternative International Economic Strategies and Their Relevance for China*. The World Bank, Washington, D.C.

Skarlicki, D.P., Folger, R., 1997. Retaliation in the workplace: The roles of distributive, procedural, and interactional justice. *J. Appl. Psychol. 82*, 434–443.

Social Insurance Law, 28 October 2010. *Social Insurance Law of People's Republic of China*. Presidential Decree of the People's Republic of China (No. 35), Beijing.

Spector, P., 1997. *Job Satisfaction: Application, Assessment, Causes and Consequences*. Sage, Thousand Oaks, California.

Steers, R., 1977. Antecedents and outcomes of organizational commitment. *Adm. Sci. Q. 22*(3), 46–56.

Stone-Romero, E.F., Stone, D.L., 2005. How do organizational justice concepts relate to discrimination and prejudice?. In: Greenberg, J., Colquitt, J.A. (eds.), *Handbook of Organizational Justice*. Erlbaum, Mahwah, NJ. pp. 439–467.

Storey, J. (ed.), 1995. *Human Resource Management: A Critical Text*. Routledge, London and New York.

Streek, W., 2011. Taking capitalism seriously: Toward an institutionalist approach to contemporary political economy. *Socio-econ. Rev. 9*, 137–167.

Tang, T.F. (ed.), 2017. *Annual Report on Shenzhen's Labor Relationship (2017)*. Social Science Academic Press, Beijing.

Tang, T.F. (ed.), 2018. *Annual Report on Shenzhen's Labor Relationship (2018)*. Social Science Academic Press, Beijing.

Tepper, B.J., 2001. Health consequences of organizational injustice: Tests of main and interactive effects. *Organ. Behav. Hum. Decis. Process. 86*(2), 197–215.

Tobin, D., 29 June 2011. Inequality in China: Rural poverty persists as urban wealth balloons. BBC, https://www.bbc.com/news/business-13945072 [accessed 20 March 2020].

Tokman, V., 2007. The informal economy, insecurity and social cohesion in Latin America. *Int. Labour Rev. 146*, 81–107.

van Dierendonck, D., Schaufeli, W.B., Buunk, B.P., 2001. Burnout and inequity among human service professionals: A longitudinal study. *J. Occup. Health Psychol. 6*(1), 43–52.

Walton, R., 1985. From control to commitment in the workplace. *Harv. Business Review 6*(3), 60–66.

Walumbwa, F.O., Hartnell, C.A., Misati, E., 2017. Does ethical leadership enhance group learning behaviour? Examining the mediating influence of group ethical conduct, justice climate, and peer justice. *J. Bus. Res. 72*, 14–23.

Wang, T.X., 2017. Strong grassroots organizations and working force is the root of trade unions' early intervention in labour dispute. In: Tang, T.F. (ed.), *Annual Report on Shenzhen's Labor Relationship (2017)*. Social Science Academic Press, Beijing. pp. 147–156.

Warner, M., 2011. Labour markets in China: Coming to terms with globalization. In: Benson, J., Zhu, Y. Y. (eds.), *The Dynamics of Asian Labour Markets: Balancing Control and Flexibility*. Routledge, London and New York. pp. 134–147.

Warner, M., Zhu, Y., 2018. The challenges of managing 'new generation' employees in contemporary China: Setting the scene. *Asia Pac. Bus. Rev. 24*(4), 429–436.

Webber, M., 2012a. *Making Capitalism in Rural China*. Elgar, Cheltenham UK.

Webber, M., 2012b. The dynamics of primitive accumulation: With application to rural China. *Environ. Plan. A 44*, 560–579.

Webber, M., Zhu, Y., 1995. Export processing zones in East Asian development. *N. Zealand J. East. Asian Stud. 2*(2), 73–90.

Webber, M., Weller, S., O'Neill, P., 1996. Participation in labour adjustment assistance. *Economic Labour Relat. Rev. 7*, 295–324.

Whitfield, K., 1987. *The Australian Labour Market*. Harper and Row, Sydney.

Wial, H., 1991. Getting a good job: Mobility in a segmented labour market. *Ind. Relat. 30*, 396–416.

Wilkinson, F. (ed.), 1981. *The Dynamics of Labour Market Segmentation*. Academic Press, London.

Williamson, O.E., 1979. Transaction-cost economics: The governance of contractual relations. *J. Law Econ. 22*, 233–261.

Womack, J., Jones, D., Roos, D., 1991. *The Machine That Changed the World*. Harper Perennial, New York.

Wong, C., 1995. *Fiscal Management and Economic Reform in the PR China*. Oxford University Press, New York.

Workplace Testing, 2019. Job Stress, 26 April, https://www.workplacetesting.com/definition/360/job-stress-workplace-health [accessed 22 April 2019]

World Bank, 1988. *China: Finance and Investment*. The World Bank, Washington, D.C.

World Bank, 1994. *China: Foreign Trade Reform*. The World Bank, Washington, D.C.

World Bank, 1997. *China Engaged: Integration with the Global Economy*. The World Bank, Washington, D.C.

Wrest, S. 2017. Trade union law and collective bargaining in China, *China Business Review*, 21 April, https://www.chinabusinessreview.com/trade-union-law-and-collective-bargaining-in-china/ [accessed 24 April 2020].

Wright, I., 2005. The social architecture of capitalism. *Phys. A 346*, 589–620.

Wright, I., 2008. 'A closed social architecture model', Paper presented at the conference 'Probabilistic Political Economy: "Laws of Chaos" in the 21st Century', 14-17 June, Kingston UK: Kingston University, http://staffnet.kingston.ac.uk/~ku32530/PPE/wright.pdf [accessed 19 December 2013].

Wu, X.W., 2017. Building comprehensive pilot district for harmonious labor relations in Guangdong: Exploration and practice. In: Tang, T.F. (ed.), *Annual Report on Shenzhen's Labor Relationship (2017)*. Social Science Academic Press, Beijing. pp. 19–27.

Xie, Y.H., Zhu, Y., 2016. Holding up half of the sky: Women managers' view on promotion opportunities at enterprise level in China. *J. Chin. Hum. Resour. Manag.* 7(1), 45–60.

Yang, B.H., 2017. Thinking about building harmonious labor relations in Shenzhen. In: Tang, T.F. (ed.), *Annual Report on Shenzhen's Labor Relationship (2017)*. Social Science Academic Press, Beijing. pp. 28–38.

Yang, G., 16 March 2017. 'China employee social insurance: Make your payments in full'. China Law Blog, https://www.chinalawblog.com/2017/03/china-employee-social-insurance-make-your-payments-in-full.html [accessed 24 April 2020].

Yang, H.Q., 1995. *Banking and Financial Control in Reforming Planned Economies*. St. Martin's Press, New York.

Zen, S.K., Zhou, X.Z., 2017. Research and prospect of Shenzhen's social insurance development under supply-side structural reform. In: Tang, T.F. (ed.), *Annual Report on Shenzhen's Labor Relationship (2017)*. Social Science Academic Press, Beijing. pp. 64–81.

Zen, X.H., 2017. An analysis of enterprise workers' salary level in Guangdong province. In: Tang, T.F. (ed.), *Annual Report on Shenzhen's Labor Relationship (2017)*. Social Science Academic Press, Beijing. pp. 50–63.

Zen, X.H., 2018. Research on the wage income gap in Guangdong. In: Tang, T.F. (ed.), *Annual Report on Shenzhen's Labor Relationship (2018)*. Social Science Academic Press, Beijing. pp. 70–81.

Zhang, Y., 3 March 2019. 'China to introduce policies to lessen burden on businesses and individuals'. the State Council of PR China, http://english.www.gov.cn/premier/news/2019/04/03/content_281476593332672.htm [accessed 2 January 2020].

Zhang, Y.Z., 18 March 2019. *'Beijing: Industry, economics, and policy'*. China Briefing, https://www.china-briefing.com/news/beijing-industry-economics-policy/ [accessed 6 November 2019].

Zhu, Y., 1995. The function of special economic zones in East Asian development. *Asian Economies 24*, 26–49.

Zhu, Y., Warner, M., 2004. Changing patterns of human resource management in contemporary China. *Ind. Relat. J. 35*, 311–328.

Zhu, Y., Warner, M., 2018. Managing "new generation" employees in China and beyond: Summing-up. *Asia Pac. Bus. Rev. 24*(4), 578–584.

Zhu, Y., Webber, M., 2017. Impact of western economics on China's reforms from the late 1970s to the present: An overview. In: Warner, M. (ed.), *The Diffusion of Western Economic Ideas in East Asia*. Routledge, London and New York. pp. 348–359.

Zhu, Y., Sardana, D., Cavusgil, S.T., 2020. *Weathering the Storm in China and India: Comparative Analysis of Societal Transformation Under the Leadership of Xi and Modi*. Routledge, London and New York.

Zhu, Y., Warner, M., Feng, T.Q., 2011. Employment relations with "Chinese characteristics": The role of trade unions in China. *Int. Labour Rev. 150*, 127–143.

Zhu, Y., Webber, M., Benson, J., 2010. *The Everyday Impact of Economic Reform in China: Management Change, Enterprise Performance and Daily Life*. Routledge, London and New York.

Index

accountabilities 83
administrative employees 32–3
administrative reforms 13
advanced manufacturing systems 14, 19
affective component 64
age: and co-worker support 102; and
    employee commitment 103; and
    employee satisfaction 98, 99; and
    equivalent pay optimism 116; and
    future employability 114, 122; and
    future training expectations 113, 122;
    and future work effort 112, 121; and
    future working conditions 112, 117,
    122; and health 96; and job control
    101; and job security 108, 118; and
    pay raise optimism 111, 118; and
    perceived distributive fairness 74–5;
    and routinization 101; and stress 97;
    and supervisor support 102; and
    willingness to quit 103
agent-based models 131–2
All China Federation of Trade Unions
    (ACFTU) 13
alpha coefficient 85–6
arbitration system 17–8
attitudinal commitment 84

behavioural commitment 84
behavioural component 64
Beijing 5–6, 29, 37, 73, 77
career development 51–3

causal workers 23, 25, 29, 30, **40**, 42, 136
Central Party Committee 12
certification: and co-worker support 102;
    and employee commitment 103; and
    employee satisfaction 98–9; and

equivalent pay optimism 123; and
    future employability 114, 122; and
    future training expectations 113, 122;
    and future working conditions 112,
    117, 122, 123; and job control 101;
    and job security 108, 118; and pay
    raise optimism 118, 121; and perceived
    distributive fairness 75, 76; and
    perceived interactional fairness 77;
    and routinization 101; and stress 97;
    and workloads 100
chaotic conditions 133–9
'China Dreams' 25
China Labour Statistical Yearbook 128–9
citizenship: and co-worker support 102;
    and employee commitment 103; and
    employee satisfaction 99; and future
    employability 114; and future training
    expectations 113; and future work
    effort 121; and future working
    conditions 112, 117; and health 96;
    and job security 108, 118; and pay
    raise optimism 118; and perceived
    distributive fairness 75; and stress 97;
    and willingness to quit 103
cognitive component 64
collective agreements 35–6
collective bargaining 13
commercial banking system 12
Commission for Restructuring the
    Economy 13
commitment; *see* organizational
    commitment
'comprehensive inspection campaign' 16
conceptual framework 2–3
'continuation of class struggle' 12
contract workers: commitment 103;

employee satisfaction 77, 98, 99; equivalent pay optimism 116, 123; experiences by, vs. dispatched workers 46; on future employability 114; on future working conditions 117, 123; health 96; job control 101; perception of distributive fairness 74; stress 97; willingness to quit 103; workloads 100
core process 136–41
cost of living 4
co-worker support: measurement scale 87; in new era 84; research discussion 101–2
'cradle to the grave' mentality 3
'Created in China' 19
CVs 134, 136–7, 138

disabled workers 22
dispatched workers: commitment 103; co-worker support 102; employee satisfaction 77, 98, 99; experiences by, vs. contract workers 46; on future training expectations 113; on future working conditions 112; health 96; managing 37; pay raise optimism 111; perception of distributive fairness 74; perception of routinization 101; recruitment and treatment of 29–31; stress 97; supervisor support 102; varying coverages for 33–4, 50; workloads 100, 121
disputes *see* labour disputes and unrests
distributive fairness or justice: concept discussion 61, 62, 63; research discussion 73–6; survey questions **66–7**
DPEs (Domestic private enterprises): adoption of modern management systems 39; communication with management 54; employee satisfaction 78, 99, 100; employees' income concerns 48; employment contracts 50–1, 51; equivalent pay optimism 116; future employability 114; future working conditions 112, 117; job control 101; job security 108; overtime work 49; pay packages 49; perceived distributive fairness 76; promotions 52; supervisor support 102; training 53, 113; workloads 100, 121

economic profile of selected regions **6**
economic reform: first three decades of 12–4; introduction 1–3; *see also* labour management; policy reforms
economy of labour: chaotic conditions 133–9; complexity, embedding and forms of allocating labour 131–3; conclusion 142–3, 153–4; demonstration and implications 139–42; described 135–9; introduction 126–7; labour market theories 127–31
econo-physics 131–2
education: and co-worker support 102; and employee commitment 103; and employee satisfaction 78, 98–9; and future training expectations 122; and future work effort 121; and future working conditions 112, 117; and health 96; and job security 108; and perceived distributive fairness 75, 76; and routinization 101; and stress 97; and supervisor support 102; and wage 20–1; and willingness to quit 103
employability, optimism about 114, 122
employee commitment *see* organizational commitment
employee participation 34–5, 83, 152
employee satisfaction: conclusion 152–3; and relationships 83–4; research discussion 77–8; research results **69–71**, **147–8**; survey questions **67**; with work, research discussion 97–100; with work, research results **89–95**
employees: causal 23, 25, 29, 30, **40**, 42, 136; negative effects of reforms on 4; new types of 28–31; non-local resident 29–31, 33–4, 50; overall response to reforms 24–5; *see also* contract workers; dispatched workers; employees' experiences and responses; migrant workers
employees' experiences and responses: career development 51–3; conclusion 54–60, 150; employment contract changes 50–1; introduction 45–6; key changes 46–9; pay packages 49; relationships with management 53–4; summary of responses **55–8**, **146**; *see also* employee satisfaction; fairness, perception of; optimism; well-being
employers: defined 134; overall response to policy reforms 24; *see also* economy of labour; management initiatives
employment contracts 50–1

enterprise, government policy influence on 27–8; *see also* management initiatives
enterprise autonomy 12
equality theory 63
equity theory 63
experience and wage 20–1

fairness, perception of: concepts discussion 62–4; conclusion 78–80; data used in analysis 64–5; employee satisfaction 77–8; introduction 61–2; research results **68**, **69**–71; research themes and questions **66–7**; *see also* distributive fairness or justice; interactional fairness or justice; procedural fairness or justice
female workers; *see* gender
FIEs: adoption of modern management systems 38–9; collective contracts 35; communication with management 54; employee participation schemes 35; employee satisfaction 78, 100; employees' management concerns 48; employment contracts 51; equivalent pay optimism 116; future employability 114; future working conditions 112, 117, 122; overtime work 50; pay packages 32–3, 33, 49, 151; perceived distributive fairness 76; promotions 52–3; supervisor support 102; training 53, 113; workloads 121
'five insurances and one housing allowance' 23
Fixed-term Contract Employment 12
flexibility, increased focus on 4
Foreign invested enterprises; *see* FIEs
formal markets 130
Foxconn 19, 137
future expectations; *see* optimism

gender: and co-worker support 102; and employee commitment 103; and employee satisfaction 98, 99; and equivalent pay optimism 123; and future employability 114, 122; and future training expectations 113; and future working conditions 117, 123; and job control 101; and job security 108, 118; and pay raise optimism 118; and routinization 101; and stress 97; and supervisor support 102; and willingness to quit 103; and workloads 100, 121

Gini coefficient 1, 61
government agencies, familiarity with 72–3
graduates, assistance for 22
Guangdong 5, 15, 20, 35, 52
harmonious labor relations 14–5
health **88**, 96–7; *see also* well-being
Hebei 5, 6
high-tech companies, non-use of dispatched workers by 30
housing allowances 23, 33–4, 50, 151
hukou status: and co-worker support 102; and employee commitment 103; and employee satisfaction 99; and equivalent pay optimism 116, 123; and future employability 114, 122; and future training expectations 113, 122; and future working conditions 112, 117, 122, 123; and health 96; and housing allowance 23; and job security 118; legislation protecting women 12–3; non-local resident workers 29–31, 33–4, 50; and pay raise optimism 118; and perceived distributive fairness 75; and routinization 101; and stress 97; and supervisor support 102; and willingness to quit 103; and workloads 100, 121; *see also* migrant workers
Human Resource and Social Insurance Department 24, 25
Hunan 5, 6, 52
immediate environment 137–41
informal markets 130
inspections 16, 17
interactional fairness or justice: concept discussion 62, 64; research discussion 76–7; survey questions **67**
interest rates, lowering of 19, 24
'internet + professional training' 22
'iron-rice bowl' mentality 3, 4

jiancha daxingdong 16
job control: measurement scale 86; research discussion 101
job opportunities: research discussion 100–1; and routinization 83
job security 108, 118
job stress: causes and effects of 82; measurement scale 86; research discussion 97
jobs-for-life principle 12
Joint stock companies; *see* JSCs

Joint ventures 48, 54
JSCs: communication with management
54; co-worker support 102; employee
commitment 103; employee
satisfaction 78; employees'
management concerns 48;
employment contracts 50; equivalent
pay optimism 116, 123; future
employability 114, 122; future work
effort 112, 121; future working
conditions 112, 117, 122, 123; health
of workers 96; job control 101; job
security 118; overtime work 50; pay
raise optimism 121; perceived
distributive fairness 76; promotions
52; routinization 101; stress levels 97;
supervisor support 102; training 53,
113, 122; willingness to quit 103
justice; *see* fairness, perception of
JVs 48, 54

labour allocation 131–3, 139, 141
Labour Contract Law 35, 36
labour contract system 17
labour disputes and unrests: and
collective agreements 35–6; initiatives
for managing 12–8; new challenges 18;
and trade unions 25
Labour Law 13
labour management: impact of reforms
on 3–4; summary of findings 144–50,
145–9; *see also* policy reforms
labour market theories 127–31
'labour situation information sharing
platform' 17
labour supply: new employee types
28–31; shortages in 18–20
life expectancies 6
Likert scale 86
local workers 75
location: and co-worker support 102,
112; and employee commitment 103;
and employee participation 152; and
employee satisfaction 77, 98, 99; and
equivalent pay optimism 114–6, 123;
and future employability 114, 122; and
future training expectations 113, 122;
and future working conditions 112–3,
117, 122, 123; and health 96; and job
control 101; and job security 108, 118;
and pay raise optimism 108, 118; and
perceived distributive fairness 73–4;
and perceived interactional fairness

77; and perceived procedural fairness
67; and routinization 101; as
significant determinant 124; and stress
97; and supervisor support 102; and
willingness to quit 103; and workloads
100, 112–3, 121
macro-economic reforms; *see* policy
reforms
macro-equilibria 132
'Made in China' 19
male workers; *see* gender
management initiatives: adoption of
modern management systems 37–9;
collective agreements 35–6; conclusion
39–44, 150; employee participation
34–5; and future expectations by
employees 124–5; government policy
influence 27–8; introduction 27;
managing different employee types
36–7; pay packages 31–4; promotion
34; recruiting new employee types
28–31; summary of managers'
responses **40–2, 145–6**; summary of
new initiatives **145**
managerial positions: employment
contracts for 51; and wage 21
Marxist labour market theory 126, 140
mediation system 17–8, 25
men; *see* gender
micro-economic initiatives;
see management initiatives;
micro-equilibria 132
migrant workers: assistance for 22;
discrimination against 124; non-
receipt of many benefits 25; perception
of distributive fairness 75; supervisor
support 102; *see also* citizenship;
see also hukou status
minimum wages: and *Labour Law* 13;
and labour supply shortages 19; in
Shenzhen 17
Ministry of Labour 13
modern management systems 37–9

non-local resident workers 29–31,
33–4, 50
north *see* location
objective procedural justice 64
occupational certification;
see certification
older workers 4, 22
Open Cities 12
Open Regions 12

opportunities *see* job opportunities
optimism: about current job over next
five years 107–13, **109–11**; about
employment elsewhere 113–7, **115**,
116; about job relative to others
117–23, **119–20**; conclusion 125, 153;
impact of reforms on **148**;
introduction 106–7; and management
124–5; and policymakers 123–4
organizational commitment: concept
discussion 84; impact of reforms on
148; measurement scale 87; research
discussion 102–3
organized markets 130
overtime pay: in Beijing 31; disparities in
151; in Shenzhen 15–6; unrest
concerning 14

pay packages: employees' responses
regarding 49; management incentives
31–5; *see also* wages
People's Commune system 12
performance: employees' responses
regarding 47–8; increased focus on 4;
and pay 31–3
'Plan of Improving All Citizens'
Skills' 22
policy reforms: conclusion 25–6; impact
on labour management 3–4,
144–50, **145–9**; implications for
employers and employees 23–5;
introduction 11; labour supply
shortages 18–20; managing disputes
and unrests 12–8; managing social
insurances 22–3; productivity and
well-being 20–2; *see also* employees'
experiences and responses;
see also management initiatives;
see also summary of findings
primary markets 130
procedural fairness or justice: concept
discussion 62, 63–4; research
discussion 65, 68, 72–3; survey
questions **66**
production workers 32
productivity and well-being 20–2
professional certification *see* certification
professional qualifications and wage 21
promotion: employees' responses
regarding 51–3; varying criteria for 34,
52–3, 151–2
provinces in sample 5–6

*Provision Concerning the Administration
of the Labour Market* 13
*Provision of Settlement of Surplus
Labour* 13

regions in sample 5–6
relationships and job satisfaction 83–4
research methodology 4–8
respondents, profile of 7–8
responsibilities 83
responsibility system 12
robots 19
routinization: measurement scale 86;
and opportunities 83; research
discussion 100–1
'rule of law' 17, 28, 42, 54, 149, 155
rural citizenship *see* citizenship
sales employees: high turnover rate
among 37; pay packages for 32
sample 5–8
satisfaction *see* employee satisfaction
secondary markets 130
sectors and wages 20, 21
senior managers 32–3
SEZs 12
Shenzhen 15–8, 23, 25
*Shenzhen SEZ Owed Wages Guaranteed
Regulation* 16–7
Shijiazhuang 30
short-term fixed contracts 12
single-party-ruled societies 155
social environment 138–41
social inequality 1
Social Insurance Law 22–3
social insurances: employers' response to
24; managing 22–3; varying coverages
for 33–4, 50, 151
social stability 14–5
'socialist economic construction' 12
'socialist market economy' 4
SOEs: adoption of modern management
systems 38–9; collective contracts 35;
communication with management 54;
employee commitment 103; employee
satisfaction 78; employees' income
concerns 48; employment contracts
50, 51; equivalent pay optimism 123;
future employability 114, 122; future
work effort 112, 121; future working
conditions 112, 123; impact of reform
on 3, 12; job security 108, 111;
overtime work 50; pay packages 33,

151; pay raise optimism 108, 111; perceived distributive fairness 76; pre-reform 3; promotions 52–3; supervisor support 102; training 53, 113, 122
south *see* location

Special Economic Zones 12
state-owned enterprises; *see* SOEs
stress *see* job stress
subjective procedural justice 64
summary of findings: conceptualization of labour management and markets 153–4; conclusion 154–6; introduction 144; issues for future research 155–6; labour management 144–50, **145–9**; pay and working conditions 151–2; responses to reforms 150; well-being, satisfaction, equity, and future expectations 152–3
supervisor support: measurement scale 86–7; in new era 84; research discussion 101–2; *see also* interactional fairness or justice

tasks 83
taxes 19, 24
technicians 32
technology usage 22, 24
Temporary Measures on Collective Wage Consultation 13
tenglong huanniao 19
tenure and wage 20–1
'*The Everyday Impact of Economic Reform in China: Management Change, Enterprise Performance and Daily Life*' 11
Trade Union Law 13, 36
trade unions: collective agreements 13, 35–6; and company size 36; firm-level roles of 25
training: disparities in 151; employees' responses regarding 51–3; future expectations on 113, 122; for older workers 4, 22
turnover rates 37

unemployed people 22
unorganized markets 130
unpaid workers 142, 154
unrests *see* labour disputes and unrests

urban citizenship *see* citizenship

Vice Minister of Human Resource and Social Insurance 14–5
volunteer workers 142, 154

wage gap 20–1, 151
wages: and employee type 30–1; equivalent pay optimism 114–7, 122–3; factors influencing 20–1; and inflation 48; legislation on 13; ongoing challenges 151–2; pay raise optimism 108, 111, 118, 121; performance-based 31–3; in Shenzhen 15–7; unrest concerning 14; *see also* fairness, perception of; minimum wages; overtime pay
Wages Guaranteed Fund 16
weiwen 14–5
welfare 4
well-being: conclusion 104–5, 152; data and scales used in analysis 84–7; introduction 81; physical and psychological aspects of work 82–4; and productivity 20–2; research discussion 96–103; research results **88–95, 147**; research themes and questions **85**
willingness to quit: defined 84; measurement scale 87; research discussion 102–3
women; *see* gender
work, physical and psychological aspects of 82–4
work overload; *see* workloads
workers, defined 133; *see also* economy of labour; *see also* employees
working conditions: future expectations 112–3, 117, 121–2, 122–3; management initiatives 33–4; ongoing challenges 151–2
working hours: employees' responses regarding 49–50; and gender 75; management initiatives 33
workloads: change in 83; future expectations 112, 121; measurement scale 86; research discussion 100–1
wuxian yijin 23